A Little Fruitcake

A Little Fruitcake

A Childhood in Holidays

DAVID VALDES GREENWOOD

Da Capo Press
A Member of the Perseus Books Group

Designed by Timm Bryson
Set in 10.75 point New Baskerville by The Perseus Books Group

Cataloging-in-Publication data for this book is available from the
Library of Congress.

First Da Capo Press edition 2007
ISBN-10: 0-7382-1122-2
ISBN-13: 978-0-7382-1122-0

Published by Da Capo Press
A Member of the Perseus Books Group
http://www.dacapopress.com

Da Capo Press books are available at special discounts for bulk
purchases in the U.S. by corporations, institutions, and other
organizations. For more information, please contact the Special
Markets Department at the Perseus Books Group, 2300 Chestnut
Street, Suite 200, Philadelphia, PA, 19103, or call (800) 255-1514
or e-mail special.markets@perseusbooks.com.

1 2 3 4 5 6 7 8 9

For my brother, Ignacio,
who endured me

Contents

fruit•cake (frōōt´·kāk) *n.* 1. A heavy, spiced cake containing nuts and candied or dried fruits. 2. *Slang.* A crazy or an eccentric person: *"a fruitcake under the delusion that he was Saint Nicholas."* (John Strahinich)

—from *The American Heritage Dictionary, Fourth Edition*

I

The Powder Keg
Under the Tree

As I held the foil-wrapped shoebox in my hands, I could hardly breathe. I was five years old, possessed by a question of life-or-death importance: would my present cry or wouldn't it?

The package in my hands was the culmination of my life's work, or so it seemed in 1972. I had put in my request in November—not of that year, mind you, but a month before the *previous* Christmas. The fact that my request had already gone unfulfilled for one holiday is telling. Even at five, I knew that if the box in my hands contained what I dreamed of, then I had accomplished a feat even grander than talking my grandmother into letting me stay up late to watch *A Charlie Brown Christmas.*

November 1971 marked the first holiday season since my mother had left my Cuban émigré father in Miami and returned home to rural Maine, where she'd been raised. After apartment life in Boston and then the Little Havana section of Miami, we found ourselves living in a real house like nothing my brother, Ignacio, and I had seen before.

Over two hundred years old, my grandparents' house was constructed in New England farmhouse colonial style: a shed attached to a building that housed the porch and kitchen, which was then attached to a two-story structure housing the bedrooms, dining room, and living room. It looked like many of the houses in Norridgewock, Maine, which is to say, like a fat white caterpillar whose segments were punctuated with doors and windows. There was an earthen cellar below, where Grammy kept all her canning, and a newspaper-lined attic over the shed that we used as a garage. We had two deep wells for water and an enormous garden outlining the backyard in an L-shape. About the only thing reminiscent of Miami was the clothesline strung from the shed to an ancient maple, the shirts and sheets flapping in the wind just as they had on the lines in Little Havana.

When Mom moved back into her parents' home with my older brother and me, she was forcibly returning Grammy and Grampy—both shoe shop workers on the brink of retirement—to a life they were sure they had left behind: child raising. But they managed to adapt with equanimity, turning the spare room into a bedroom for two boys and setting an elderly swing set on the once-unspoiled front lawn.

One of my earliest memories at Grammy's house is of that first Thanksgiving. All the grown-ups had gathered in the living room late in the afternoon, and "Uncle" Howard asked me what I wanted for Christmas.

Uncle Howard was one of many not-really-related-to-us aunts and uncles in our lives. On Thanksgiving, with the few adult-sized chairs taken, he sat on an ottoman made by Sister Lee from church. This nifty footstool was really just three metal milk cans covered in colorful fabric and dressed up with pom-pom fringe, a very low post that put him much closer to my height than the other adults. I could look him in the eye as I answered eagerly: I wanted a baby doll.

Who knows where that came from? My playmates were all other boys. I can't picture taking anyone else's baby doll for a spin only to decide I needed one of my own. Maybe I saw a newborn baby somewhere, and thought, Surely there must be a plastic version out there for little boys like me.

It's a better bet that I saw a doll while watching television. Despite being devoutly religious, our family nonetheless watched a lot of television. The afternoons were a smorgasbord of what Grammy called "my stories." It is odd that soaps were so beloved by a woman who objected to her grandsons' seeing *Batman* reruns (too violent) and, a few years later, *Wonder Woman* (outfits too skimpy). Day in and day out, once Grammy finished her chores, she and Mom took up their stations in the living room, juggling *Days of Our Lives, All My Children, One Life to Live, Edge of Night, Search for Tomorrow,* and *General Hospital,* a feat that required missing half an hour of one soap to catch the last half-hour of another. Perhaps sandwiched between the antics of evil Phoebe Cane or nice Nurse Jesse, I saw an ad for a baby doll.

All I know is that my desire was clear and my answer so primed that it burst out without hesitation, silencing a roomful of grown-ups who had been enjoying the tryptophan stupor of their Thanksgiving feast. Did they laugh? Did they ask me if they had heard correctly? I remember a hiccup of silence and a vague awareness of some disapproval—not surprising since every person in that room went to our church. We were fundamentalists who (despite our obsession with television) eschewed a host of sinful activities from drinking to dancing to playing cards. The tenets of our faith most certainly did not include encouraging boys to play with dolls, but if anyone said so that afternoon, I don't recall it. My clearest impression is of having made my request.

As far as I knew, it was a done deal. I didn't doubt for a second that I would get a doll that Christmas because, from the moment my brother and I had come home to Maine from Miami, relatives and friends had fawned over us as if we had just splashed down safely after a mission to the moon. In my innocence, I believed that only a matter of weeks stood between me and the baby doll of my dreams.

I was mistaken in this regard. My brother and I each got the exact same five gifts: a blow-up octopus, the powdery smell of which still lingers in my memory; a metal train; a plastic snowmobile; a helicopter; and a mechanical dog that barked. In a photo of that Christmas, Ignacio and I sit on my bed, side by side, with our matching bowl cuts and new toys gathered around us. There is no doll.

Had I known then that this would be one of my family's most flush holidays, and thus this trove of gifts was the grandest it would ever be, I probably would have appreciated my new toys more. True, I enjoyed them well enough, considering that they were merely diverting second-choice gifts. I especially liked the dog, which I played with so often that it eventually began to lose its battery-operated bark, emitting only a slurred mewling noise. But a dog was no doll—and this was a problem.

I dug in. That March, when my fifth birthday—St. Patrick's Day—approached, I announced to anyone who would listen that I wanted a baby doll. Instead, I got a green cake and a toy truck, which I eyed suspiciously. When my mother's birthday came around in July, I asked her what she wanted, though only as a pretense to tell her that if I were in her shoes, *I'd* want a doll.

One late summer afternoon, after an excursion to Frederick's Dar-I-Whip, I sat in the backseat of my mother's 1969 AMC Rebel, sucking down a milkshake and only half listening to her conversation with a friend sitting in the passenger seat. My ears started to burn when I heard the friend say, "So give him the doll."

I'd missed whatever my mother had said first, but I wanted to jump up and down as the friend continued.

"It's the seventies. Lots of boys play with dolls now. It's not going to make him—" And here she trailed off, only belatedly considering the little pitcher with big ears. I saw her looking in the rearview mirror, and she saw me seeing, then dutifully told my mother that I might have caught the gist of this exchange. My mother muttered, "Shoot," with the resignation of one who knows she is up against the stubborn will of a child with a one-track mind.

I wasn't all that concerned with the words left unspoken by my mother's friend. Whatever a doll would or wouldn't make me, I cared only that someone had registered a vote for my wish. Now my countdown to days of glorious pretend burping and feeding could begin in true earnest.

Grammy, it turns out, was less keen on this progressive "go with the times" logic and had said so. But Mom went ahead that December and bought a baby doll anyway, then waited until the last minute to admit it. Ever a woman unafraid of expressing her very firm opinions, Grammy was furious. Her anger was not something to be taken lightly. Though just a few inches over five feet, she was a large woman in those days, her body thick and almost squared off, like a Russian farmworker in a textbook. This was in the years of roller curls, before perms became the fashion, and her hair—a white halo as fixed and unmovable as she was—simply added to the effect of her power. Her eyes, a nonthreatening gray-blue most of the time, seemed to darken visibly when she was mad, narrowing into glittering slits of anger, as they must have at my mother's pronouncement.

How could my mother possibly pull such a stunt right under her nose? How could Mom just ignore Grammy's values while yet basking in the glow of her charity? What did she want her son to become, for heaven's sake?

I overheard this exchange from my perch at the top of the living room stairs. Our house had its share of quirky details. The stairs to the unheated upper bedrooms were attached to one wall of the living room, built with no divider and only much later hemmed in by a wooden railing to keep family members from plummeting parlorward. The couch with the best view of the television was backed up against these stairs, so that if its occupants were sufficiently engrossed in their program, a little boy could huddle on the top step unseen when he was supposed to be asleep in bed. Bracing myself against the wall like someone trying not to fall off a ledge, I watched many programs I wasn't supposed to. After months of practice, I could be deathly quiet and hold this pose for a good half-hour without tumbling into view.

The *Sonny & Cher* show was on that night. Let me count the ways I loved Cher. I loved her hair, which was shinier than any I'd ever seen, even our neighbor

Barbie's, whose hair was pretty good by the standards of the real world. I also loved Cher's laugh, which was husky and deep, like a smoker's (but without the yellow teeth). I loved how she got all the good lines, and Sonny just had to stand there hiding behind his mustache. Considering that their show never aired before my bedtime, I shouldn't have even known Cher existed, but my grandfather loved variety shows and had made *Sonny & Cher* a fixture on his viewing schedule. I had the top step all to myself when Grammy found out what I was getting for Christmas—and erupted.

My mother's defense was weak ideologically and grand strategically: the present was already wrapped.

Grammy was not impressed. "I guess I can just about figure out how to solve that!"

But my mom persevered. "He's already seen it. What if he's picked it up? What if we switch it, and he knows?"

What if, indeed. I *had* picked it up, and I *would* know if they switched it. Just a few nights before, while Mom was out of the house and Grammy was cooking dinner, I had waited until Grampy was "resting his eyes" during the evening news, then crept over to the tree. There were four or so gifts with my name on them, one of them so soft it couldn't be my baby, and another, too small. I knew that one of the remaining boxes was from Miami, where my father lived, and let me be clear: there was no way a Cuban *papi* in 1972 was giving his son a doll. That left a present the shape and size of a shoebox.

When I picked up the box for examination, it made a little sound: a half-cry, cut short when I dropped the box, sure that the noise would rouse Grampy. I backed away from the tree as fast as I could, exultant in my discovery. Not only had they gotten me a baby doll, but they'd gotten one that cried. The luxury!

I was understandably horrified, then, to discover that this might not actually be the present I was to receive. If Grammy put her foot down, seeing as she was the ultimate grown-up among grown-ups, able to make all manner of relatives bend to her will, who knew what I might find in that box come Christmas morning. A ball? Another truck? A squirt gun? *Sonny & Cher* was no consolation that night as I realized my dilemma: little boys who aren't supposed to know what they're getting for Christmas can't exactly protest the unfairness of not getting something they haven't yet *not* gotten.

What was the big deal? This question plagued me in the days leading up to Christmas. It clearly had something to do with my being a boy, but I didn't know what. I asked my brother if he would play with a doll, and he just made a face that said, "I can't believe you asked that. You are *so* five." Part of me didn't want to want something that would meet with such overt disapproval from both my brother and Grammy, but that reluctance was no match for my desire. I wanted that doll, and I didn't want to have to wait another year for it.

I turned this over and over in my head as I played "Icicle Show," a new game I had invented. I would steal lengths of silver tinsel from our tree and lay on the floor next to the forced-air heating grate, waiting for the furnace to kick in. I'd hold a shiny strand over the grate, and every time a blast of air came up, I'd let go of the tinsel to see how far the hot air could lift it. There was an element of performance art to this. The grate was directly in front of a mirror, which meant that the Christmas tree behind me was also reflected in front of me, yielding an effect in which I felt completely immersed in the glow of colored bulbs. If I tossed a whole handful of silvery strands into the airstream at once, they would spread all over me as they slowly fell to earth. If you looked in the mirror at that precise moment, it was like a scene in a holiday snow globe, and I was the chubby little figurine enjoying the glittery storm.

With hindsight, I can only imagine how that looked to Grammy. If I could turn heating equipment into a fabulous showcase for theatrical play, well, then just imagine where a baby doll might lead. Later, when I was old enough to understand how people perceived and treated effeminate boys, I would understand Grammy's anxiety better. But that year, I was simply a five-year-old innocently pondering his baby doll while listening to Cher. And Grammy wasn't having it.

Christmas morning, then, was a powder keg. Had she pulled off a switcheroo while I slept? Would I have to fake being happy with whatever nonbaby thing was in that box? Or would I find a doll in there after all? Would I spontaneously combust while waiting to find out?

In those years, we still opened presents in the morning. The Christian world is thus divided: there are those who want their loot before bed and those who want to wake up to it the next day. Despite the fact that Grampy and Grammy both would have preferred to be Christmas Eve people, we waited until the morning of the twenty-fifth because of someone's errant notion that this is what children expect. Though we would've been thrilled to open the gifts at the first possible opportunity, we dutifully went to bed present-free so we could wake up to discover whatever delights awaited.

That morning, Grampy was nursing the first stages of a chocolate migraine. Despite the fact that chocolate gave him blinding headaches that sent him to bed for half a holiday at a time, he received boxes of bon bons by the sleighful every Christmas—not because anyone wished him skull-rattling pain and near blindness, but because chocolate was the gift he himself asked for every year. His grown children, fellow churchgoers, and coworkers obliged, figuring that if he wanted the candy, its effects couldn't be that bad. They were wrong, but only those of us who lived in his house were exposed to his increasing levels of grumpiness and irritation, followed by his moans, and then his absence for hours. As always, not feeling obliged to wait for Santa, Grampy had already opened a Whitman's sampler the night before, and thus began Christmas day in his chair with jaw clenched and eyes half closed.

Ignoring his pain, Mom put a Grants department store holiday album on the record player to get us in the mood. We boys knelt by the fake cardboard fireplace Grammy set out for Christmas every year, and as we waited for her to pass out the presents, I tried to remain calm. Grammy's eyes were narrowed, and her lips were set in a tight line as she handed out the first gifts. Perhaps just to be done with the whole drama—to which only my brother was oblivious—she gave me the shoebox straight away. She didn't say a word, and I swear there was a hush in the room.

Gift in my grasp at last, I could have ripped the wrapping paper off instantly, but I knew that would only have revealed a box underneath still to be opened. That wasn't fast enough for me: the quickest way to know what was inside was to just flip the box over and see if it still cried.

It did—and I wanted to cry as well.

The sheer relief of knowing that, yes, I had gotten the doll made me light-headed. The paper finally came off, the shoebox lid was removed, and there it was: a baby, very bald and all mine.

Who knows what I (or anyone else) got that Christmas. I was busy exploring my new companion. The doll had no hair, real or painted on, so it was clearly a *baby* baby, which I loved. Baldness notwithstanding, I knew by its gorgeous, slightly alien eyes that it must be a girl. The molded plastic of its face featured deep cutouts for startling eyes made of what looked like green glass. Silken auburn eyelashes were affixed to lids inset in the plastic. If I held her a certain way, those freaky eyes would languorously shutter themselves, only to reopen slowly when righted, a feat she repeated over and over again at my will. Oh bliss!

Dolly, a name that came to me in a burst of clear and deeply original inspiration, was dressed. She wore a little two-piece outfit that was soft and pink. And in the way. I began pulling it off immediately, determined to wrap Dolly in a blanket, like a newborn was supposed to be. (If swaddling was good enough for Baby Jesus, obviously it was good enough for Dolly.) But as I pulled off the top, I made a discovery that was a brief source of disappointment: Dolly cried whenever she was not on her back.

I'm sure the designer's logic was that if, say, a little Cher fan turned the doll face down and heard it cry, he would instinctively soothe the doll by rocking it, face up, in his meaty arms. But I had decided that babies were to be held to your chest, head on your shoulder, for soothing. I'd long had visions of myself walking around with Dolly in this position, patting her back and being a good little mother boy. Clearly, this would not work: my imagined comfort position would actually make Dolly cry incessantly until I gave in to the position she was designed to prefer. In the spirit of adaptation, I nestled my new babe in the crook of my arm, telling myself I liked the resulting Mary-in-the-manger effect. I decided that maybe the baby was better this way after all.

Without thinking, I headed up the stairs, oblivious to the fact that everyone else was still gathered around the tree.

"Where do you think you're going?" asked Grammy, spoiling for a fight.

I paused, wondering how she could even ask such a thing. "I'm going to get Dolly a blanket so she won't be cold." I sounded aggrieved, as if I had not myself just denuded the poor thing, and I gestured toward the frosted windows as if to illustrate the danger.

"It's *winter*." I climbed the last steps until I was just out of sight, but I waited a moment, at the top of the stairs, and heard Grammy turn on my mother.

"Well," she said, "you went and did just what you wanted, didn't you? Now look at him." Grammy couldn't have hidden her disgust if she tried, and, really, she wasn't trying.

I clutched Dolly closer and headed into my room. It was a new and strange feeling that washed over me: the simultaneous sense of being both happy and sad. Grammy had succeeded in casting a pall over my delight, leaving me a little ashamed at how much I already loved my doll. I decided to take my time finding just the right blanket for Dolly.

I couldn't have known then that I would spend the next few months slowly driving Grammy insane on this topic, first by requesting a dress for Dolly, then extending that request to include a matching outfit for me. There was no way for me to know that, sure of my future ruin, she would eventually just trump my mother by taking the doll away and, in return, presenting me with a new set of bedsheets covered with NFL team logos (not that I knew what the NFL was).

But that all happened later. On Christmas morning, I chose Dolly's swaddling with great care. I rejected my first choice, a pillowcase, because it was the right size but not soft enough. I passed over my favorite flannel pajama top as well, which was soft but had buttons, too rough for a baby's skin. In the end, I took the cozy purple bedspread off my bed and wrapped Dolly in it, despite how the fabric trailed to the floor. I lifted my baby to my shoulder and let her cry for a bit, then rocked her to stillness. "*I* love you," I told her, as if to make her feel better about her rough welcome into the world.

I knew that I should go back down to join the others and that the longer I didn't, the madder Grammy would be. But it was my job to watch out for Dolly, protecting her from the mockery of my brother, the dismay of Grammy, and even the chocolate-fueled crankiness of Grampy. And as long as I stayed in my room, Christmas would remain whatever I wanted it to be. Everything else could wait.

2

Bad to Santa

What is growing up but a succession of moments when you understand that you have been missing out on important information that older, wiser people already know? That singsong rhyme you learned turns out to be an alphabet. Your books sound the same every time because those squiggles by the pictures are actually words that you can spell using that alphabet. Many such discoveries lead to proud displays of newfound knowledge and accompanying parental praise. But not every childhood epiphany is so obviously welcomed.

Such is the case with the understanding that Santa may not be real after all. It is perfectly clear to most children that the grown-ups around them are invested in the success of this charade, perhaps because so many youngsters remain deeply attached to the tale. For children who figure the whole thing out, this may present the first ethical dilemma of their young lives: Is it right to play along with the ruse in order to protect others' feelings? What should you do when "honest" and "good" aren't the same thing?

I liked to think of myself as a good boy. In fact, I actively cultivated this notion, playing up the contrast between my cherubic demeanor and my older brother's devil-may-care attitude. He was not himself a demon spawn, but he just couldn't keep a lid on behaviors that were sure to set off Grammy. For starters, Ignacio was more likely to sass back to her, a bad idea, full stop. But he was also much more likely to follow every exciting, adventurous impulse that beckoned him with promises of immediate delight, only to yield trauma and punishment later.

One year, the impulse was to take a sled up onto the porch roof, then ride it unintentionally over melting snow directly through our picture window onto the card table where Grammy did her puzzles. As many gallons of glass-studded snow poured onto the table, Grammy, immune to shock at my brother's antics, simply put her hands on her hips and complained, "That was a fifteen-hundred-piece puzzle!" Even the window disaster, however, was no match for Ignacio's eventual masterpiece, which would involve an abandoned shack, a match, several fire trucks, and a hasty retreat to our bedroom.

And where was I during these misadventures? When Ignacio was up to no good, I was most likely where I was every afternoon: curled up on the couch with my mom, as snug and harmless as a chick in a nest. When he plunged through the porch window, I just stepped back in awe to admire the colliding forces of falling grandson and fuming grandmother. And while he was discovering his inner pyro, I was reading. When Grammy asked if I knew where Ignacio had been, I touted my own benign behavior in my shameless reply.

"My book is really, really good, so I didn't even notice that he was gone until he ran in like he did, and I heard all the sirens."

The truth is, I was no angel—I just knew how to maintain my halo in the presence of others. I was ever tempted to break rules set for me about what I could and could not do. And though I remained obedient most of the time, my "good" behavior was a reflection not of moral superiority but rather of a healthy instinct for self-preservation. If I thought I would get caught at something illicit, I just didn't do it.

If I could get away with something undetected, though, I was all over it. One gorgeous day, for instance, I had sassed back to Mom, who grounded me in the house, barring me from a moment's play outside. But as soon as she left on an errand, I bolted through the front door, aware that Grammy had not caught wind of my grounding. Another time, I had been told to stay out of the plastic wading pool in our backyard, but waited till Mom and Grammy were sucked into their soap operas to wade in anyway, figuring that water, being invisible, would leave no tell-tale traces on my skin when I headed inside to join them later.

Partly because of the opposing nature of our sins, with me breaking mere rules and my brother breaking actual buildings, and partly because I so actively cultivated the notion that I was an innocent boy, Ignacio and I were seen very differently; poor guy, he was trouble, and I was sweet. Only one other person in the world knew the truth about me: Santa Claus. Or, to be more precise, Not Really Santa Claus.

By the time I was six and a half, I didn't believe in Santa. The Santa story came with holes in it from the get-go, such as his tardy appearance long after the gifts had appeared under our tree. Moreover, I think Grammy had some misgivings about actively participating in such a clear falsehood, even a nice one; thus, she spent very little time reinforcing belief in jolly Saint Nick. But all that paled in comparison with a bigger issue: Wasn't Christmas about the baby Jesus, anyway, and not the goings-on in an imaginary North Pole? Santa was clearly an add-on, one who was fun and made for great animated specials, but still . . . .

So, when my brother, hoping at the advanced age of eight to spoil the tale, came to me that year and said, "You know Santa's just made up," I shrugged.

Well, duh. You might think my refusal to be wowed by Ignacio's big revelation would have been a huge disappointment to him. Instead, it acted as a true source of bonding. If neither of us believed in Santa, we could put up a united front against all those silly adults who thought that any kid growing up in the frozen climes of Maine would ever be stupid enough to buy the notion that a fat old man could survive an entire December night outside in an open sled wearing only felt. It was a kind of power, our disbelief, and in its thrall, my brother and I could be a team, at least for a season.

Our shared wisdom united us, even as we kept mum about it. Though we scorned neighboring children who believed this nonsense, we agreed not to mock them to their faces. When April, the girl next door, talked about staying up to see Santa when he landed on her roof, Ignacio and I smirked quietly. When Peter from across the street headed indoors from playing in the snow every afternoon so that he wouldn't miss the half-hour television show in which Santa claimed to be broadcasting from the North Pole, we didn't question his devotion. It was better simply to bask in the smug knowledge that we were so much more mature than our friends. We didn't have to rub their little baby noses in it.

Beyond that, we somehow instinctively knew that bragging about disbelieving in Santa was not an endearing quality around the holidays. We neither wanted to send a friend home in tears, with his psyche forever scarred, nor to suggest to our own family that we were ungrateful smart alecks. Instead, Ignacio joined me in my fakery as we "good little boys" made it clear to the adults that we were very eager to see what Santa would bring us.

This playacting seemed perfectly fair: if grown-ups pretended to believe in Santa, so could we. No one got hurt, everyone got presents, and we all won. It was the earliest example in my life of how some lies are actually considered okay. I would soon notice other proofs of this, like when Grammy's sister Marion asked how she looked, and Grammy praised her. Once my great aunt had left, Grammy went on to call Marion's hair a bird's nest. She was lying about her real opinion but had decided that engaging in a wee bit of falsity was a nicer way of treating her sister than invoking the Audubon Society to her face. Apparently, everyone agreed that the maxim "honesty is the best policy" didn't apply to bad hair or men in red flannel suits.

With everyone playing dumb, I could have my cake and eat it, too, I reasoned. I didn't believe in Santa as fact, but I enjoyed him quite a bit anyway. I liked his rich red suit, the idea of a flying sleigh, all those adorable reindeer, and the elves, who seemed so light in their pointy loafers. And I had even gotten hooked on the Santa show, long on cheer and short on production values, which involved lots of cardboard and a hand puppet or two. For one thing, I liked it because I felt in the know: while most kids were sitting at home trusting this portly pretender, I knew the score. He would say that he had a letter from a Mike or a Betty, and he knew whether these children had been naughty or nice, and this alone was meant to be convincing. By the time he said he was reading David's list,

I just rolled my eyes. In the 1970s, Davids were like milkweed pods: we sprang up everywhere. In a school so small that there were only fifty kids in ten grades, I was one of three Davids—and not the only one in my class. Santa was going to have to do better if he wanted to convince me.

Did this keep me from writing him a letter? Not at all. I wrote a "Dear Santa" missive in block letters, enjoying the ritual but not expecting that I would actually receive, say, a real elephant. When my mother asked me if I wanted to mail the letter to the address on the TV screen, I wasn't sure what to make of it? Did *she* believe in Santa? Had my brother not clued her in? Or was she just telling the big lie, too? Not sure if I was protecting her innocence or acting as an accomplice in her deception, I simply handed the letter over. It seemed the right thing to do.

It was one thing to watch the Santa show at home, where I could be alternately entertained and jaded. It was another thing entirely to encounter Santa face to face. I could have played along, displaying my Holiday Angel side, but instead my Inner Smarty Pants took over. And is there a Santa on earth who likes a Smarty Pants?

Late one afternoon, the week before Christmas, my mother, Ignacio, and I were at the bank in Skowhegan. It was not our bank, the little one in Norridgewock where my brother and I each had savings passbooks we didn't quite understand. Mom had heard that Santa was making appearances at the bank in the next town, close to LaVerdiere's Super Drug Store. Seeing as Ignacio was eight and I was six, old enough by 1970s standards to take care of ourselves, Mom dropped us off at the bank to visit Santa while she ran to LaVerdiere's. Can there be a sight more frightening to a hired Saint Nick than a parent receding into the distance without her children in tow?

My brother and I didn't even have to talk about what to do. There was something unspoken in the air, a whiff of polyester wig perhaps, that made us hungry, like wolves following deer. Maybe it was the fact that this jolly old soul lacked a bowl full of jelly, his belt cinched around a narrow waist. Or that the slip of elastic connected to his beard was clearly visible over one ear. The nerve of this man to think we could be so easily fooled! We waited until the few other children in line had left, then cornered our prey.

"Are you the real Santa?" Ignacio asked innocently.

"Well," Not Really Santa said nervously. "Do *you* think I'm Santa?"

Wrong question. "I think that the real Santa is going to be at the North Pole today," I said, laying my cleverest trap.

"That's right," Not Really Santa said, relaxing a little. "I will be."

Ignacio pounced. "He didn't say *you* would be. He said *Santa* would be."

"But I *am* Santa. I'll be at the North Pole tonight!" Not Really Santa was trying, god bless his hopeless soul.

But I was ready.

I pointed at the big bank clock. "Santa will be broadcasting his TV show from the North Pole in ten minutes. How are you going to get there in *ten minutes?*"

Not Really Santa now understood, both from my schoolmarm tone and the I'm-going-to-eat-you shine in our eyes, that there was no hope of salvation.

"Well, if you don't really believe in Santa . . . "

"I believe in Santa, but you're not really Santa, are you?" I asked, smelling blood.

Before Not Really Santa could reply, Ignacio jumped in. "Or are you saying the *other* Santa isn't real?"

"Well . . . "

Ignacio kept on him.

"Or are you *both* fake?"

I moved in for the kill.

"Why would you pretend to be Santa if you're not?"

It was pure evil, what I was doing. Here was this nice man trying to bring a little joy to the world (and perhaps sign up a few new checking accounts), and I was badgering him like he was a common criminal on the stand. Moreover, I was accusing him of being the fake version of something I didn't believe in by comparing him to another version I had already written off as fake in the first place.

"You two move along now." Not Really Santa's voice was tight and decidedly lacking in cheer.

"Yeah," Ignacio said. "We better go, or we'll miss the *real* Santa on TV."

"Just move along." And just like that, Santa turned his back on us, without offering so much as a "ho, ho, ho" or a candy cane for the trip home.

With a last, gloating "Bye Santa!" we headed out the glass door into the parking lot. Admittedly, this wasn't our finest moment as young citizens. But for brothers more prone to sabotaging each other than to teamwork, our wicked romp was a brief moment of true bonding. For the rest of that season, we remained united in our efforts to keep all the grown-ups assured of our belief.

When Mom pulled up, and we climbed into the backseat, she asked how Santa was. We kept our answer neutral.

"He was okay."

And then we grinned like madmen all the way home.

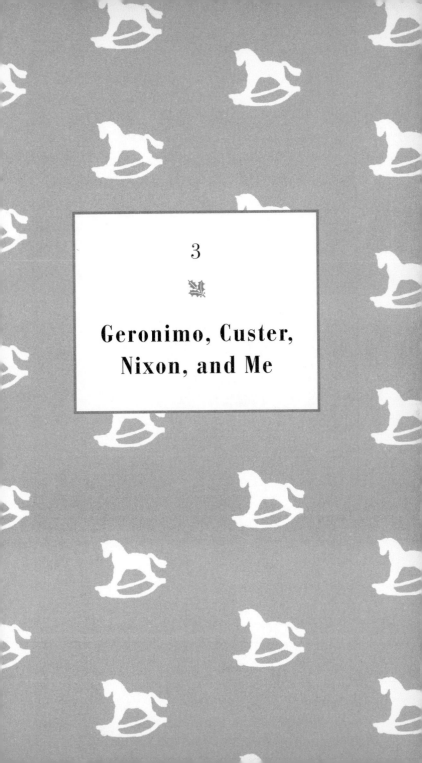

3

Geronimo, Custer, Nixon, and Me

Christmas came early in 1974. Really early, especially if you were a kid. A few days before Thanksgiving, we got some serious snow. By serious, I mean almost three feet in forty-eight hours. As the sky remained dark and heavy, globs continued to pelt the windows hour after hour, and the grown-ups all got nervous, imagining just how they would dig out of this mess. Meanwhile, we kids grew ever more excited. As a seven-year-old, I was in no danger of having to shovel the driveway; all I knew was that once it stopped snowing, the white expanse would truly live up to the term *winter wonderland*, a landscape for playing in, on, or under.

Of course, the days of fun ahead were premised on the snowfall actually stopping. On the second day of the storm, with no letup in sight, Grampy and Grammy bundled themselves into stiff winter coats and thick wool hats to dig a path from our front door to the street. This was no easy task as they first had to get the door open with two feet of heavy snow packed against it. Across the street, old Mrs. Hamilton was chipping away at her own knee-high wall of white. I sat on our staircase, taking in the scene through the living room window: grown-ups in front of every house shoveling as fast as they could in hopes of returning their driveways to view, even as the snow continued to fall and the storm-thick skies stayed dark. It was an epic task, one that the shovelers seemed to conduct wordlessly, while I kept cozy inside and listened to a stack of Grant's Christmas albums.

The next morning, the sun peered down at us through a thick gauze curtain, revealing yet another foot of accumulation, obscuring the previous day's labors. Three feet of snow is a lot, but when added on top of nearly a foot of existing snow, then pushed to even greater heights by the snowplows that passed up and down our street, the result was transformative. The houses on the block suddenly looked smaller and closer together. The first holiday lawn ornaments of the season had disappeared entirely under snow cover, as had the last remaining bikes of the most stubborn kids. The shrubs and tree stumps that marked the topography of our neighborhood had been reduced to mere contours. Best of all, the windows were covered up to the halfway point by the new drifts.

This was not an unusual occurrence in those years. For several winters running, we had received enough snowfall to encase the entire first floor of each house on the block for a few days at a time. Most years, though, we didn't approach that benchmark until February. To get three feet of snow toward that goal all at once, not only before the New Year but before Christmas, was an incredible boon for us kids.

If kids in Maine know anything, it's how to play in snow. Once the snow was more than a couple of feet deep, we would dig tunnels from house to house, a workout surpassing anything that summer required of us. Using just our mittens and maybe a small hand shovel, we burrowed through hard-packed snow, carving out round pathways just nominally bigger than ourselves. The paths were almost all horizontal, so we could wriggle and snake our way forward from destination to destination, often tumbling out the exit hole on the other side in a heap. Occasionally, we'd make forts big enough to stand up in, but mostly we focused on a serpentine network of tunnels entirely invisible from above. What must it have been like for our parents to look out their windows and see nothing but unbroken whiteness and think to themselves, *Well, they must be in there somewhere.*

The down side to tunnels was obvious: collapse. I hated being halfway to the exit hole at the next house only to have the snow pile in on me. Getting a mouthful of snow wasn't the worst trauma ever, but if it was unexpected, it made me panic a little bit; I'd wriggle backwards as fast as I could to escape and not, as I could picture all too well, end up buried till spring.

We didn't play on top of the snow around our house much, seeing as that would have risked our stepping on a tunneling friend's head just below the surface. If we wanted to cross over the snow, instead of burrow through it, we were likely to do so in the field running behind all the backyards on our street. Because the field was wind scoured, the snow was never as deep. The few kids who had snowshoes used them there; several of us strapped on tennis rackets for the same effect, and we swore it was just as good. (It wasn't.)

But there was no better way to approach snow than from above. By "above," I mean from the rooftops of our houses, where we kids were allowed to play when the snow was especially deep. Grammy had even set rules for it: we could play on the rooftops, *but* if even a sliver of light peeked through the big window on our porch, it was game over. Ignacio and I considered ourselves lucky because the guy who plowed our driveway usually banked the snow by the porch, helping to cover the wide picture window sooner than nature alone would allow. The banked snow made it a breeze to climb up to the top, where we'd wander around proudly at perilous heights. That year, with so much snow so soon, was going to be an exceptional one for playing on the roof.

But we couldn't start immediately. One blizzard hadn't been quite enough to block the window completely, and things cleared up for Thanksgiving Day.

While the rest of the world dug out from the blizzard, that weekend Grammy and Mom had decided to take

Ignacio and me snowsuit shopping in the nearby "city" of Waterville. A college town of twelve thousand with a dozen restaurants and not one, but two, shopping plazas, we thought it a true metropolis, For one thing, compared to Norridgewock, Waterville was on the cutting edge of Christmas light technology, with house after house outlined in brightly colored bulbs, many set to automated flashing patterns. My favorite display had crossed candy canes blinking on the lawn, tall snowmen flanking the home's front steps, and a set of reindeer, lit from inside, that appeared to be lifting off for flight. Heading into Waterville so soon after the big snowstorm, we found the reindeer and bulbs alike buried, their lights shining through the crust of snow the way glaciers glow from within.

At Rich's Department Store, Mom and Grammy scouted the racks in search of snowsuits, while I openly gawked at "the city folk." Look—a woman with Christmas tree earrings and green eye-shadow! Over there—a guy with hair as long as a Breck girl's and tiny little eyeglasses! Grammy admonished me to stop staring at strangers and pay attention to the suits she had found: mine burgundy and Ignacio's navy. We didn't even take the time to try them on; we just stood still in place while Mom held them up in front of us to see if they fit. It was decided that we would get the same size, despite the fact that Ignacio was eighteen months older and two inches taller than I was. Having looked at the smaller snowsuit for me that Mom held up first,

Grammy bit her lip before announcing, "He'll never fit into that thing. No toothpick, that one."

To her way of thinking, the extra material intended for length would be pulled upward to accommodate my noticeable width, and that would balance things out. She was pretty close to right. I didn't care because this was a marvel of engineering: the entire thing was one piece, its single zipper running from foot to neck, with a hood and gloves that snapped on at thick rivets, encasing the wearer in a storm-fighting bundle of impenetrable fabric.

I couldn't wait to get home, despite the fact that it was too late to play in the snow. I just wanted to try on my snowsuit, which I did, only to encounter a side effect of the fierce fabric. It was *loud*. The material was so stiff that it would not be enough to say that it crinkled when I walked. It was more like the sound you'd make when vigorously sanding old paint off metal. It gave me the shivers, so I pulled the hood up over my ears to mute the noise. That helped, and my happiness with my new purchase was restored. The rich red color also distracted from my miserable winter boots; while the other kids had cool snowmobile boots with jazzy stripes of color, Ignacio and I wore the same felt-lined rubber boots that Grampy and ancient Eldon Lee from church wore. Our new hi-tech playsuits more than made up for our embarrassing footwear.

Every snowfall over the next few weeks got us closer to the goal of roof time, and soon enough we were scrambling up over the eaves. By Christmas, a half-dozen kids were perched on our rooftop for their first jump of the year. You see, it wasn't really the rooftop that was the ultimate goal: it was snow-jumping *off* the rooftop. Jumping is a core ingredient of childhood, after all. In the spring, we jumped into puddles barefoot, making the biggest splash possible. In the summer, we jumped out of trees and into ponds. In the fall, we made enormous leaf piles to jump into after a running start. But nothing matched snow-jumping for the pure rush. The distance from roof to snowbank wasn't typically enormous, but the view from up high made it feel more dangerous, and my heart raced during the brief fall to the snow below.

Most of the kids' roofs were sharply pitched peaks lined with corrugated aluminum, a New England architectural detail intended to keep buildings from collapsing under the weight of accumulated snow. The combination of steep angle and slippery surface made it almost scarier to ascend the roof than to leap off it. Compared to most houses, our porch roof was angled at a gentle pitch, and the snowbanks were piled so close to the eaves that the whole experience was perfect for my comfort level. I could live a little dangerously, but only a little. I didn't have to be a true daredevil to take the plunge.

After Christmas, though, the stakes were raised as the drifts grew even deeper. People began taking photographs of the drifts to send to relatives out of state as proof that we weren't exaggerating about the snow. Christmas trees set out for removal poked out of drifts so far off the ground that they appeared to float above the street. By the week of New Year's, our little roof was no longer excitement enough, and someone suggested we jump from the tallest house on the street instead.

At three full stories, the Gardiner house seemed to tower on its lot. Of all the neighborhood kids, only I had ever been inside; Peter Gardiner and I were the youngest kids on the street, so we ended up playing together a lot. It was up to me, then, to ask his family if we could go up on their roof. It wasn't a task I relished.

I shuffled noisily up their stairs in my snowsuit—scrape, scrape, scrape—dreading whom I would find. Luckily, Peter's Grandpa, who was generally uninterested in kids' nonsense, answered the door. I bravely made my request. I think his exact words were, "I don't care what you kids get up to as long you don't make a lot of ruckus."

So it was that we kids, not having alerted any parents to our plans, found ourselves in the attic of the Gardiner house, stepping out onto the roof, one at a time, for the snow jump of all snow jumps. Because the sun sets so early in the winter in Maine, it was already getting dark by the time we started jumping. Ignacio's best friend, Darren, went first, and he slipped a little on the roof. He said the F-word, as I called it, which both scandalized me and made me nervous. I was beginning to regret this choice of venue, so much higher than what I was used to, but everyone else seemed excited. When Darren leapt, he yelled "Geronimooo" to much cheering and applause; Ignacio followed suit with a cry of "General Custer!" I realized I needed to quickly come up with not only the nerve to make a leap but some signature action on top of it.

I decided to do my Nixon wave.

It had been a big deal in our house on the late summer day a few months before when Nixon left office. On a perfectly sunny afternoon, everyone had come inside and stood in the living room, silently glued to the images on the screen of Nixon walking away from the White House. When I asked what was going on, Mom explained that the president was giving his job to the other guy on the screen. When Nixon climbed the steps of the helicopter, I asked where he was going, and Grammy simply said, "Away, I hope."

The meaning of the moment was lost on me, but the way it had stopped everyone cold in his tracks made its magnitude clear. When the guy who had just given away his presidency waved farewell, his wave was so big, so over the top, he was like a cartoon character saying goodbye. I fell in love with that gesture—it was so outsized and dramatic. One arm covered half his face as the wave began and then he swung wide, ending with a two-hand salute, which I thought looked like the peace symbol that I'd seen hippies flash on the news. Arms wide over his stiff body, Nixon was a grinning, human letter Y. He might have been losing his job and going away, but he sure didn't look sad about it.

I had practiced that wave countless times since, and it always cracked adults up. I didn't know why exactly, but I loved earning a big laugh, so I kept it up. That wave was to be my big dismount from the third-story rooftop at the Gardiner's house, except that as soon as I stepped onto the pitch, I lost my footing and fell over. (This was a move more Ford than Nixon, not that I or anyone else yet knew it.) Somehow, I ended up on my back, head down, and that is the position I remained in as I slid along one of the aluminum grooves and shot off the rooftop into the cold air. Two stories is a long way to fall, especially if you are upside-down, and I screamed the whole way. I must have made quite a picture: a fat red bullet plummeting toward the snowbank as my friends scattered to avoid being crushed.

Ignacio ran over and stood above me, his breath frozen into long plumes as he asked if I was all right.

"Of course, I'm not," I said, furious, and painfully rolled myself down the snowbank to run home. I registered in the back of my mind that no one was pursuing me, that despite my obvious near-death experience, those damn fools were heading back inside to jump some more.

When I burst into the house, crying about my fall, Grammy and Mom were in the middle of preparing dinner. They could hardly make sense of what I was saying, but it seemed to me that they got the gravity of the situation right away as they both paled visibly. For a moment, I could see them looking at each other for help, as if conspiring about how to solve a problem that seemed to have something to do with my snowsuit. It took a moment before I had any idea what they were looking at; I blame this lag in my recognition of the true situation on the fact that I was numb with cold from playing outside all afternoon. But as the warmth of our woodstove brought feeling back to my limbs, I discovered what they had seen immediately upon my entry: the fancy new snowsuit had been no match for the hearty corrugated roofing. The raised groove that had guided my downward trajectory had also slit open my snowsuit from butt cheek to heel. And as soon as the blood had returned to my frozen limbs, it pushed outward through the new cut, tracing the line where the snowsuit had split. The screaming mess I had been when I walked through the door was nothing next to the banshee I became when I could finally feel the three-foot-long boo-boo on my backside.

That winter Grammy added a new rule to the snow-game restrictions: no one was ever allowed to play on the Gardiner's roof again. I didn't need the rule. Think of it as the first New Year's resolution of my life: I wasn't going to snow-jump ever again. Period. I would still play outdoors all winter, but I'd confine my adventures to harmless snow tunnels. Granted, I couldn't show off my Nixon wave in the narrow icy burrows, but since I also never emerged wounded from a snow tunnel, I considered the trade-off a blessing.

4

Jealous of
Baby Jesus

The same year as the big snowfall, many Christmas stories competed for my attention, most of them television specials with singing and dancing clay figures. A wise second-grader, I knew these were silly made-up stories, but I found little kernels of reality in some of them. *The Year Without a Santa Claus* might as well have been a version of my family photo: plump, melodramatic Heat Miser standing in for me; skinny, aggrieved Cold Miser for Ignacio; and Mother Nature, sweet on the surface but controlling all nature with her iron fist, for Grammy. Even better was *Rudolph the Red-Nosed Reindeer,* in which a deer who is bad at sports and a little elf who has great hair run off together to find out where they belong.

Yet, no matter how deep my love of these stories, nor how thoroughly I had memorized their folksy musical numbers, not one of them remotely approached the narrative power for me of what Christians call the Nativity story. I was a little bothered by the word "nativity"—what on earth did it mean? Something about natives?—but I found the tale itself thrilling. When I thought of poor Mary, my mind went straight to this one expectant mother in my church, her belly big in front of her, who groaned softly every time she settled onto one of the hard century-old pews. If sitting on those pews was uncomfortable, what must it have been like for Mary to ride on a bony donkey? And worse, since the story was always told in December, I projected a Maine winter onto the streets of Bethlehem; I could just see Joseph leaning into the wind of a winter's night, realizing he could no longer feel his cheeks.

At last, so the story went, one sort-of-kind soul took pity on the exhausted couple, offering up a stall for them to camp out in. I lived in rural Maine, and I could picture this all too well. On Jack Hicks's farm, the stalls were coated with a mixture of dirty straw and cow poo, and they smelled. Christmas carols all ignored this icky reality and instead focused on the word "manger," which sounded kind of nice. At age seven, I had never heard "manger" used in any other context but the Nativity, so when I finally realized that it meant "trough," I felt a little nauseous. Mary and Joseph not only had to make their camp in poo, the only place for their baby was a stinky box that cows stuck their dripping noses into.

Yet all that dreariness was the perfect set up for the big finish: the Nativity drama came with a happy ending in which a huge starburst announced the baby's arrival, angels sang, shepherds ditched their dim livestock to see what the fuss was about, and even kings dropped whatever royal-type things they were doing and rode camels all the way to Bethlehem for the baby shower. Cosmic eruptions, heavenly choirs, and expensive presents—Baby Jesus had it made.

For a hammy kid intent on crowd pleasing, this really was the greatest story ever told: the night that a little boy made the whole world watch. Secretly, shamefully, I had to admit that I was jealous of Baby Jesus. I knew it was crazy to wish that I could be the star of such a scene, when the Cute Kid to end all Cute Kids had already been born two thousand years before I arrived ready for my close-up. Yet I just couldn't help wonder what it would feel like to have all eyes on me like that.

The closest approximation of such adoration that I'd seen firsthand had been in Miami—and it wasn't for me. In Miami, my brother enjoyed the role of First-born Son. In Cuban culture, this made him a rock star; relatives fawned over Ignacito, "little Ignacio," whose existence was the proudest accomplishment of big Ignacio, our father. While people praised and flattered my brother, I was a mere redundancy, just the chubby other son. If I wanted any sort of residual afterglow from the light shining on Ignacio, I had to tag around after him, something he rarely allowed me to do.

Back home in our small town, there was definitely no such Firstborn Son privilege for Ignacio. In fact, because I carefully maintained my Good Boy status, I was the favored one much of the time, at least with Mom. Grammy, however, was too old to indulge either of us with any kind of coddling.

Grammy fawned over just one person: my Uncle Russell. Neither the youngest nor the oldest of five children, he was clearly the apple of Grammy's eye nonetheless. She referred to him as "my baby" and swelled with special pride at the mention of his name, despite the fact that his other siblings weren't exactly chopped liver: one brother was a police chief, another was a pastor, and the older sister owned a jewelry store. Though Grammy was proud of them all, there was something about Russell that made her features soften and the twinkle in her blue eyes emerge.

That Christmas was one of the few times Russell came home from Tennessee. He had moved south when he was younger to marry a woman twice his age who had once been his church school teacher, a development that had crushed Grammy. With no love lost between Russell's wife and his family in Maine, when he finally came back for a visit, he came alone.

His arrival may not have occasioned an angelic host to sing, but it certainly felt like a star was shining. Grammy instantly transformed into a playful, almost girlish person, someone I had never seen before. It was a little like the moment in *Santa Claus Is Coming to*

Town when mean old Burgermeister Meisterburger is given a yo-yo and suddenly becomes a babbling boy. Grammy and Russell joked with each other like pals, and I marveled that he not only dared to tease her but that she'd just laugh, poking him and telling him to behave himself. And this seemed to cause a ripple effect. Mom was cheerful, Grampy relaxed, and a steady stream of friends and relatives came to our door, despite the still-growing drifts of snow.

Russell didn't make much of an impression on me at first. I remember him as tall, round faced, and balding by thirty—a silly putty version of Grampy, but younger and with real teeth. What won me over was a nifty feat of kitchen magic on the Saturday night of his visit. Because we were living on Grandparent Time, we had already eaten supper at four o'clock and had long been settled in for our ritualized family viewing of *Wide World of Sports*, *The Lawrence Welk Show*, and *Hee Haw*. As a grown-up living on real time, Russell was not interested in eating on the geriatric schedule, and several hours after we'd eaten, he announced that he was making pizza. Perhaps noticing that Grammy had her lips parted to protest, he added, "And if no one else wants any, the dough will keep." Only because it was Russell, Grammy closed her mouth and turned her attention back to the television. It must have been an act of supreme will for her to sit there quietly, knowing that there would soon be flour all over her kitchen after she'd already done the dishes and wiped down the sideboard.

Not finding Lawrence Welk quite as "wunnerful" as Grammy and Grampy that night, I eventually padded out to the kitchen to see what Russell was up to. The only light on was the one bulb hanging over the sink. The rest of the room receded into darkness around that small bulb's yellow halo. Russell stood with his back to me, pulling dough and punching it. When he realized I was there, he said, "Want to see something?" Without waiting for my answer, he threw the dough into the air. It slipped briefly into shadow and then wobbled back to his balled fists, which he used to catch and flip the dough onto a cutting board with a resonant slapping sound. And then he did it again. It was mesmerizing.

For such a son, Grammy had to make sure Christmas was perfect. That day, she started her work in the kitchen in the morning and then kept at it for hours. In addition to a turkey the size of a Volkswagen to roast, there were two pies to bake, Jell-O to set in a heart-shaped mold, cranberry relish to make from scratch, and a host of assorted side dishes to prepare, including the green bean casserole with French onions that she only made when we had guests over after church. Supper got pushed back all the way to the cosmopolitan hour of five o'clock to allow for a nominal compromise with relatives used to dining a little later. The house smelled like heaven to a little boy with a good appetite, and I was more than ready to eat when Grammy told everyone the food was ready.

But we were in for a rude surprise. With too many people to fit in the dining room, Grammy had set up a satellite table on the porch for Ignacio and me. This demotion to a kids' table—with only two kids, mind you—shocked me. Ignacio and I *always* ate at the real table, our assigned spots seemingly set in stone: Ignacio directly across from me, with Mom and Grampy on either end of the table, and Grammy at my side. This was the natural order, the way it should be. I started to protest, but Grammy had neither time nor interest.

"Food won't taste a bit different just for being on the porch. It's not like you can't see us from there."

And that was that.

An outrage, but I couldn't make a big stink about it, or everyone would think I was a spoiled brat—*not* my goal. Exiled to the tan folding table reserved for Grammy's puzzles, I felt as if I'd been abandoned on the island of discarded grandchildren. I brooded, and brooded some more, not that anyone noticed. I could hear the grown-ups talking over each other, their voices creating a clamor seldom heard in our house. Compared to the average *Buena Noche* celebration in Miami, this was probably a dinner party of church mice, but by Norridgewock standards, it ranked as a festive blowout. Ignacio didn't seem to care, instead fiddling with a transistor radio to see if he could find Wolfman Jack or something just as good, but I was annoyed to be so excluded. And, contrary to Grammy's claims, my green bean casserole did not taste as good as I knew it would have at the table.

I was dying to be in on the hubbub. I had to concoct a plot that would somehow display my exemplary long-suffering nature, prove that I had the holiday spirit, and earn my return to the action all at once. I couldn't whine or look petulant, for it was crucial that everyone realize for themselves that they should be including me. Then inspiration hit: I could achieve all of this with Legos.

These were old-school Legos, which is to say they were just rectangles. That's it. No curves or hinges or wheels. Making elaborate designs required cunning, skill, and a kind of imaginative blindness: you had to be willing to see the idea of a creation, not its literal squareness. Once I hit upon this idea, my cooling food was of even less interest. Leaving Ignacio and his radio, I skirted the edge of the dining room, squeezed quietly behind Mom's chair, and headed into the living room to produce my masterpiece—the first-ever Lego Nativity.

Kneeling beneath our tree, I moved presents around to create a place of honor for the crèche-to-be. Though the building process was not, as it turned out, effortless, it started out smoothly enough. The stall itself was easy to make, and I used all of my yellow Legos on its thatched roof. The manger was even easier to build, as if Legos had been designed specifically so one could construct a perfect baby-sized feedbox. The color was an issue: I knew a trough in those ancient days would have been made of wood, but I didn't have any brown Legos, so I picked metal-looking blue pieces instead. But the degree of difficulty increased exponentially from there.

For those intent on creating holiday dioramas using only rectangles, here is a partial list of the things that are impossible to replicate convincingly: angels, sheep, oxen, camels, a little drummer boy, three wise men, Mary, Joseph, and anything resembling a baby. The animals stumped me for so long that my relatives were on seconds before I had the first livestock completed. This was not good, as I needed to be done with the scene before the plates were cleared and dessert was set out; according to my plan, in that postmeal lull before the pies arrived, my family would notice what I was doing and be awed by the simple beauty of my handiwork. They would all bring their dessert plates into the living room and gather around my Nativity scene to eat. I would join them for pie and adoration, and Christmas Eve would thus be restored.

That meant I was on the clock. Fortunately, I had an epiphany; I realized that if I did not stack the Legos horizontally, but instead stood them up vertically, using their length to form legs, I could approximate living creatures. And if it could work for beasts, why not kings and shepherds? Yes, this meant that cows and wise men were roughly similar in height, but a little tinsel from the tree helped to mark the Magi as more royal.

The holy family posed a greater challenge. While it was fine for the bit players to be faceless, expression-less stick figures, I could not accept this for the leads. Joseph and Mary needed eyes, noses, and mouths, and Jesus had to be soft and sweet and babyish. The solu-tion for the first part of that dilemma waited several branches up on the tree. We had two bright-red mouse ornaments that had adorned every tree since the 1950s and were supposed to represent Grammy and Grampy. One mouse was tall and skinny, and one, short and round; in theory, the short one was Grammy, though in life, she was more physically imposing than Grampy. Beyond that, the Grampy mouse had a gold lamé fringe around his entire neck, which seemed better suited to Elizabeth-Taylor-as-Cleopatra than to Grampy, a mouse, or Joseph. I hesitated, really want-ing Mary to have the pretty necklace, but as I knew everyone would see the tall mouse as Joseph, I gave in and placed it behind the manger in the manly head-of-stall spot. I settled the shorter mouse next to it, where Mary would be, which turned out to be perfect—the Mary mouse was at the ideal height to gaze in at her babe. Not that he yet existed.

Nothing on the tree seemed a good option for Baby Jesus. Reindeer were out, as were glitter-covered bulbs. I looked at a snowman for a while, but when laid horizontally, as it would be in a manger, he appeared to be a pregnant woman. How confusing would that be? So I stole a page from the soap operas we watched and decided that just a bundle of cloth would be enough to suggest a baby. A box of Kleenex sat on the end table next to the couch, and within moments, a soft, white babe had been born and placed gently in his hard plastic crib. And once I had the Kleenex out, I expanded beyond swaddling clothes to clothes in general, wrapping Mary and Joseph in attire that resembled the drapey outfits they wore in Bible illustrations. You could hardly tell they were red felt mice at all. As a grace note, I moved a star ornament to the branch just above the scene. At last, I was done.

I was also late. When I turned to see if dessert was being served yet, I found, to my horror, that the pies had been cut long before and consumed as well. Relatives were already standing around in their we're-just-about-to-leave poses. There was no time for subtlety. "There's a Nativity in the living room," I blurted out, as if I had just myself noticed. No one heard me. "There's a *Nativity* in the *living room!*"

Not wanting to reveal my desperation, but actually desperate that someone should notice before it was entirely too late, I went straight to the golden boy. "Uncle Russell," I said. "Come see!"

Still talking to my Aunt Jean, Russell let me drag him into the living room. I pointed beneath the tree.

This is what I saw: a baby sleeping in his manger, with his mother leaning in close and his father standing tall above, while animals, kings, and shepherds stood guard in even numbers on either side beneath a perfect roof that kept out the winter winds.

This is what Russell saw: a big Lego triangle containing a dozen tall plastic block formations, some strung with tinsel, all gathered around a pair of mice and a tiny blue box stuffed with Kleenex. He was silent for a moment, working it out.

Finally, he pointed to the manger.

"It's a swimming pool, right? And that's water?" Indicating the taller pieces, he went on, "And those are palm trees around the pool?" He didn't even try to guess what the mice were.

I was mortified.

"It's a *Nativity!*" I bellowed, so aggrieved that I wanted to throw my precious scene at him, instead of showing it off.

He sat back on his heels. "Really?"

I nodded.

"With the mice from the tree?"

I answered at length, pointing out my soap opera swaddling trick and how I hoped everyone knew the big mouse was Joseph, even though it reminded me of Elizabeth Taylor. Russell rose and gestured to my aunt.

"Jean," he called, "You have to see this." That's more like it, I thought. He's impressed! "Little David made . . . a . . . a Nativity." His voice sounded a little strangled. Was he touched?

"He did what?" Jean came over and looked around the floor for evidence that Russell's claim was true. She looked right past it. "Where?" And when she saw what he had seen, she just shook her head. Clearly, she was trying to find the words to describe my efforts. I waited for her verdict, but then Uncle Russell interrupted.

"It's hilarious!" He bent down and gave me a hug. "You're hilarious!"

It is remarkable how quickly blindness can become sight. My imagination instantly stopped softening the forms and rounding the edges, all the life draining away from the shiny blocks. Suddenly, I could see that this was the homeliest, squarest, least convincing nativity scene ever. Look how tall the sheep are! Look at how tacky Joseph's jewelry is! And don't get me started on Mary's *whiskers!* Look, look, look! No, *don't.*

Just as quickly as I gained sight, I adapted to the new view and tried to play along, at least as far as Russell could tell. "It's pretty funny, huh?" I managed. "The kings are wearing tinsel!" I wasn't sure that Aunt Jean bought my act, and she didn't say anything at all, only led Russell out to the kitchen where goodbyes were being said. But I have a hunch she may have had a word with my mother along the way.

When Mom came in, I was sitting under the tree, trying to decide whether to start breaking up camels and shepherds or just to hide the entire thing under some presents and go upstairs. She took a gentle tack. "What's that, Sunshine?"

I didn't answer. She bent down.

"Is it a Nativity?"

I looked up at her, badly wanting to cry, and if I had spoken, I probably would have. I just nodded.

"Well, I think it's beautiful," she said, and I hugged her, so deeply glad she did.

5

The War
of the Fudges

He had more fudge.

There is no way those four words can convey to an outsider the magnitude of the injustice that occurred in 1975, two weeks before Christmas. The "he" in question was my brother, which immediately explains why it was a problem that he had more of anything. The fudge was not just any confection but the thick squares of primed-to-melt heaven that Grammy made herself and packed into the holiday tins she filled for every family member. These boxes were supposed to be filled equally with goodies, and yet, that December night, when she handed each of us our tins and the lids came off, it was clear that something had gone terribly awry: Ignacio had more fudge in his tin than I did.

I suppose if you are an only child, you may not immediately see the problem. But if you ever had a sibling close to your own age, you will well understand the seismic effect of this discrepancy. Giving one brother more of something than the other implies favoritism, a complete misunderstanding of sibling psychology, or just a wicked desire to start a dogfight. I wouldn't have put it past Grammy to have intentionally overloaded Ignacio's tin, as a way of balancing out how my mother always favored me, but it could just as easily have been the mere miscalculation of a woman trying to fill as many tins as quickly as possible. Whatever the reason, Ignacio and I both spotted the error right away, which he announced in a singsongy taunt: "I have more than you do. I have more than you do."

There were a number of ways to respond. For one, in church, we were taught to turn the other cheek, which in this case would have meant letting my brother taunt me even more. But a somewhat more recently written moral guide came to my mind first: Dickens' *A Christmas Carol*. I was totally hooked on the tale, especially adorable Tiny Tim, who got all the best presents in the end without ever having begged for them. And I loved how Scrooge, a man even crankier than Grammy, could become a sweetie overnight after a little heart-to-heart with a few witty ghosts.

The twin lessons of *A Christmas Carol* were instructive. First off, good boys earned presents through the sweetness of their demeanor, not through petulance. Secondly, if I was such a selfish idiot that I begrudged my brother a little extra fudge at Christmas, I was surely forging heavy chains to be dragged around in the afterlife. Because I was a good Seventh-day Adventist boy with a firm grip on the book of Revelations, I knew this chain business was only metaphoric as I would either be in heaven (and thus not chainworthy) or consumed by the fires of hell (and so unable to drag anything around anywhere). But the point was clear nonetheless: the Christmas spirit was about giving, not hoarding. Parity was not part of the program. My mandate was clear: rise above my covetousness to display the true spirit of generosity.

Except that I was eight and a classic younger brother.

"Ignacio has more fudge!"

Grammy came over and peered into our tins. Before her, she saw the fruit of many nights' labor. Hour after hour, she had worked to make chocolate fudge, peanut butter fudge, pink divinity fudge, date balls, oatmeal-raisin cookies, ginger snaps, mincemeat squares, sugar cookies, and fat popcorn balls, a trove she herself then divided up into tins, to be joined by mints, ribbon candies, and mixed nuts. The boxes were apportioned out, one each for herself, Grampy, all her nearby children and grandchildren, and her sister's family. She had put in the equivalent of a full workweek to make each of us our own individual cornucopia of indulgence, and what did I do? I skipped right past "Thank you, Grammy!" to something more like "I've been robbed!"

She examined my tin, then Ignacio's. To me, the extra piece of chocolate fudge towered like Mount Everest. Grammy was unimpressed.

"*That's* what you're making all the fuss over?"

I couldn't help myself. "It isn't fair! We're supposed to have *exactly* the same!"

White fingers precise as pinchers, she plucked the offending piece from Ignacio's tin—and popped it into her mouth.

"Now you do," she muttered past the fudge and turned her attention back to people who appreciated her.

I had no time to savor the sudden equity, for Ignacio was furious.

"That was mine!" His face was instantly red, almost visibly swelling.

"It wasn't fair that you—" I started, but he was already reaching into my tin.

"She took mine, so I get one of yours!"

At once, he had a piece of my fudge in hand. I slammed the lid on his fingers, effectively making him drop the desired bon bon.

"Mom!" I yelled.

"Grammy!" he cried.

And just like that, we got sent to bed.

Mad as we were, sleep was not in the cards for us anytime soon. My brother, hot to teach me a lesson, came up with a clever strategy while we lay in our beds.

"You want everything so equal? Let's divide everything up now, and then you'll never touch my things again, and I'll never touch yours."

I agreed on the spot, and we each listed toys the other was never to play with. This was followed by his eminently reasonable suggestion that we should extend this logic to the room itself, dividing it right down the middle.

"You're so lucky," he led me on. "The closet is in your half. I won't even be able to get my clothes out."

Smug, I feigned indifference to my good fortune and his suffering to come.

"We agreed to the rules," I sighed. "It's not my fault I get the closet." When I crawled into bed, I felt deeply superior to an older brother who couldn't figure out until too late that he had screwed up his own deal. *Fool.*

But when I got up the next morning, he demonstrated the strategic wisdom of his advanced age of ten. Before my feet hit the cold floor, he was triumphant.

"Might as well stay in bed because you can't go anywhere. The door is on my side!"

I was trapped. I had made such a big show of believing the rules to be sacrosanct that I could hardly complain now.

"I'm gonna go have breakfast," he taunted and stepped, just barely, out of the room. I could hear him waiting at the top of the stairs to see if I would break the new rules. I refused to give him that satisfaction, and after a moment or two, he descended, no doubt surprised that I really was obeying.

I sat there fuming at my own stupidity and trying to figure out a solution. My pride would not allow me to actually cross the line, so the only option was to jump from my side of the line through the doorway and not let my feet touch down until I was safely in the hallway neutral zone. But to achieve this meant I would need to jump about three feet on a diagonal and hope I passed through the doorposts instead of, say, smacking into them. I briefly considered standing on my bed, a few feet further away, and diving into the hall, but something told me that would not go well. I had no choice but to swing my arms in the biggest possible arcs, hoping for the kind of momentum that propels a desperate person across the finish line of a really competitive sack race.

Miracle of all miracles, my feet landed in the hallway, just as I hoped. But, like a pole-vaulter with no pole, my body lagged behind my legs, and my butt landed on the *other* side of the doorframe inside the room, while my head smacked the foot of my brother's bed for good measure. I was not a small boy, and my landing shook the house. From below, Grammy barked, "Whatever you're doing up there, stop it!"

My brother pushed past her up the stairs.

"You're on my half! You're on my half!"

I couldn't come up with a snappy reply, as I was busy figuring out whether my teeth and my vertebrae were all still where they were supposed to be. When Grammy figured out what had transpired—okay, I might have helped her fill in those blanks just a little— she put an end to room division that very morning.

But she couldn't put an end to the resulting competition that would now come to define our childhood. From this point on, if we could fight over something, we did, from who had the best toy to who sat where in the car, and onward to bickering infinity.

While, for us, the eruption over the holiday tins was only the beginning of a long battle, it may well have been the last straw for Grammy. Two weeks later, when we gathered around the Christmas tree, we got our comeuppance. With Grampy now retired and Grammy close to it and with Mom still working on her nurses aide training, things were tighter than they had been, and the big pile of presents that had greeted us in the first holidays had dwindled considerably. Under this tree, Ignacio and I each had three packages: two soft bundles and one firm box. We opened the soft ones first, figuring the good stuff would be boxed. The first bundle for each of us: two pairs of underwear. *Ugh.* The second bundle: thick white tube socks. *Double ugh.*

We hesitated before opening our last boxes. I made a show of starting to open my present, thinking Ignacio would follow suit and open his; then, when his gift was already unwrapped, I'd still have mine to open, which would drive him insane as I would have the final moment of Christmas glory. But he was wise to me and opened his with meticulous care, waiting me out. Seeing that he was going to beat me at my own game, I changed the rules: I opened mine with a flourish and shouted, "I got mine open first!"

It was a short-lived triumph. My gift was a boxed pastel-colored shirt and vest set. So was his. If we wanted equal, well, we got it. If there is anything two warring siblings do not want, it is the chance to wear matching outfits. There was a difference in color—my set was powder blue and his was peach—but the varied hues hardly made the outfits look distinct from each other. Add two more brothers in lavender and mint, and we could have been an act on the *Lawrence Welk Show*.

This was supposed to be a thrill? A Christmas in which we got only clothing, none of it fun, was supposed to wow us? It is remarkable to me in hindsight that Ignacio and I both managed to handle this moment with a display of gratefulness we entirely lacked the night we discovered the unequal tins. Maybe we had internalized the lessons of both the Bible and Dickens. Or maybe we just knew better than to piss Grammy off any more.

"Thank you, Grammy," I said.

"Thank you, Grammy," Ignacio said.

And we carried our equally terrible gifts upstairs to our room, silent the whole way, the fudge long forgotten.

6

King for a Day

There was a surreal quality to my playmate Darren's living room at Christmastime, or so it seemed to me. His family's tree, like ours, was covered with decorations to within an inch of its life, with all manner of bulbs, tinsel, garland, and lights doing their best to hide the green boughs beneath. I didn't mind that at all. What set my head spinning was not on the tree but underneath it: more gifts than we'd ever seen in one place before. In fact, the presents didn't fit under the green boughs, not by a long shot. They rose in a semi-circular pile, further obscuring the branches, and some packages were so big that they simply stood off to one side, like furniture with bows. When Darren excitedly rattled off what might be in this or that box, the list went on for so long I lost the power of hearing and sank into a kind of jealous deafness.

My brother and I simply couldn't keep up with such a conversation. By this point, we knew our own tree would preside over no more than three presents each.

And from previous Christmas experience, we expected two of these gifts to be deadly: socks and underwear. But it was the lure of the third gift, sometimes from Mom, sometimes from Aunt Jean and Uncle Fred, that enticed us. The year I was nine, we wanted skates. Actually, it wasn't just us: it seemed like every kid on Upper Main Street and beyond wanted skates. Winter lasts forever in the mid-Maine region, and in those years, hockey was the game of choice. We played wherever we could—from dinky ponds in frozen fields to scraggly rinks made by flooding whatever flat surface was available, including the parking lot of the one bank in town. Just as "banana board" skateboards had been the neighborhood obsession all that summer, ice skates were the all-consuming subject that winter. And it became increasingly clear that figure skates were for girls, and hockey skates were for boys.

Somehow I had managed to remain oblivious of the prevailing gender distinctions in skate preference. I wanted sleek, white, lace-up figure skates so I could be Dorothy Hamill. With her bobbed hair making her look like an adorable dancing mushroom, the tiny figure skater had won over the hearts of America with her Olympic gold-medal performance that year. I'd always looked forward to the figure skating competitions on *Wide World of Sports* even before her big win, but afterwards, I couldn't get enough of the thrilling, glittery routines. *Single axel! Double salchow! Triple toe loop!* Even the language was intriguing, full of mysterious phrases that I couldn't entirely parse, but memorized nonetheless as if they were Bible verses.

Watching the skaters on television wasn't nearly enough. Not yet owning a pair of skates, I would take to the frozen pond in the field behind our house and glide around on the soles of my shoes, mimicking all the tricks I'd seen. Again and again, I tried crouching into the sit spin known as the "Hamill camel," growing ever more frustrated because I simply couldn't get any decent spin without skates or speed. Jumps were a little easier, but I was most adept at just gliding around with my arms thrown behind and my chin stretched long before me, like a would-be medalist gaining speed in his long program. Over and over, I practiced my deep, humble bows to the stand of Indian sumacs that acted as my audience; the trees were silent, but I could hear the cheering crowds.

Ignacio and I had not been shy about announcing that we wanted skates and that all the kids were going to get them. As Christmas approached, I chatted with our playmates about the skates we expected, and one boy asked if I wanted brown or black. I announced that I wanted white, which led him to snort, "Nobody makes white hockey skates." Whether or not he was right about that, his dig had the effect of making me freeze with sudden fear: Did my family think I wanted *hockey* skates? Had I not mentioned that I wanted gleaming white boots atop razor-thin blades and not those fat-bladed brown blobs worn by bruisers who actually liked whacking people with sticks? When I pressed my brother on the subject, he just shook me off, muttering, "Hockey skates are the *good* skates."

For the second time in my young life, I woke to Christmas Day feeling awash with anxiety about what horror or delight might be under the tree for me. This time, I was just afraid that instead of ignoring my request, my family had indeed given me what I asked for—except that I hadn't actually asked for the right thing. I knew that if I got hockey skates, it would be my own damn fault for having been so foolishly inexplicit, but the knowledge of my own complicity wasn't going to change the depths of my disappointment. I'd heard the phrase "be careful what you wish for" many times, but no one had ever said, "Be careful how you word your wishes."

Unfortunately for my nerves, it would be hours before the issue could be resolved for good or ill. It was one of those rare years on which Christmas morning coincided with churchgoing, and Grammy was firm in her opinion that our presents could wait until afterwards. You can imagine how young boys, even awaiting only one good gift each, felt about this decision. But we knew better than to rile Grammy up by sharing our thoughts on the matter. And we could hardly beg her to let the family go late to the service: without Grammy, there would be no service at all.

Since the late 1950s, Grammy had been the church choir director, and her annual Christmas program was the pinnacle of her efforts. Most years, her choir performed the same holiday cantata from the 1920s. It had what I considered a clunky name: *His Natal Day*. I recognized the word "natal" from soap operas because every baby born on television seemed to end up in something called the neonatal care unit. But even if this did make sense, it still sounded off to me because I kept hearing the word "navel" instead, which I had just learned was the name for both my belly button and the boxes of oranges we bought in the school fund-raiser every year.

Despite how I felt about the title of the cantata, I loved it. It was ahead of even my favorite country albums, Dolly Parton's *Jolene* and Marty Robbins' *Gunfighter Ballads and Trail Songs*. I was drawn as much to the covers of these albums as to their content—on hers, Dolly wore a gleaming blonde wig that rose above her head like an enormous golden helmet, and on his, Marty was clad in a form-fitting black outfit, very Russian-spy-goes-Western. The cantata wasn't anything like the music in those albums. It was full of melodies from another era, often sounding like what a pianist might play to advance the plot during a silent movie.

To pull off her cantata each Christmas, Grammy pressed into service church members who otherwise did not do much performing the rest of the year. It was easiest to find women—even ones with full-time jobs, like nurse Diane and schoolteacher Patty—who were willing to add weeks of nighttime rehearsals to their schedules. Carol, June, Nancy, Wilma, Maryann, Frannie—there were always plenty of sopranos and altos to fill every solo, duet, and trio. But finding men was a lot harder. Yes, my brother and I volunteered, but as my voice had not yet broken, Grammy labeled me a second soprano, which didn't exactly help with her count.

The number of adult men she roped in each year sometimes fell as low as four: Grampy and a local social worker named Don sang first and second tenor, while wizened-looking Eldon Lee boomed out the bass part as if he had four lungs instead of a mere two. Aside from this trio of men who never missed a year, the cantata required Grammy to cajole at least one other man into carrying the baritone line for a season, typically all by himself. And because she could not abide the thought of doing her show with fewer than four men, she started pestering what she called her "fellas" right after Halloween, not taking no for an answer until she had the full complement. Sometimes, she was able to sweet-talk Frank, a burly bear of a man, into spending his nights singing phrases like "Hear the Christmas Joy-bells!" If she was lucky, she might also get Alfred, a local contractor, to park his equipment and pick up sheet music. In boom years, these two stalwarts might also be joined by Frank's son Joe, a state trooper, and Reggie, who typically preferred country guitar to choir music.

It must be noted that these were hardworking men in a depressed rural town, and they were not always keen to relinquish their free time to Grammy, but in our church, if there was a queen, it was Grammy, and at least once a year, her fellas agreed to be her loyal subjects.

Once the choir was assembled, she handled the men and the women a little differently as groups. Perhaps because the women were more proficient musically, she criticized them more directly, warning her altos that they were flat and shaking her finger at sharp sopranos. To keep the women happy despite her arch tone with them, she doled out featured parts like the jewels I thought they were. Grammy's sister Marion got all the good solos—she'd once sung in a radio talent contest, after all—but the duets and trios were sprinkled around among a changing cast of characters each year, their names written in Grammy's manuscript in ink and then crossed out whenever she felt it was warranted. If she was a little snippy with the women at times, they came to sing nonetheless, rewarded by her beaming pleasure when the concert was over.

With the men, she approached things more playfully, her complaints delivered as if by another person.

The men cracked jokes at the expense of president-elect Carter, who'd foolishly admitted to *Playboy* magazine that he had lusted in his heart, and despite the fact that Grammy had voted for Carter, she just clucked her tongue and told the fellas to behave. When the men blew their entrance on "We Come to Worship Him" for the tenth time, she'd say with almost a chuckle, "Now, you boys don't forget to come in on cue, or I'll have to come back there and sit with you!" Every number prominently featuring men had the note "Practice More" written in red ink on her copy of the sheet music, but she used gentle teasing most of the time so that no treasured male singer ever hopped back in his pickup truck and squealed away from the church for good. Though she often said at home that she had to "ride herd on those boys," it was clear that they delighted her, and she adored them.

Though the cantata had been a fixture for nearly twenty years at that point, she only occasionally added a Christmas pageant to the mix, using local kids to play all the parts in a living nativity. She didn't do this often because, as she put it, "I don't have time for all that nonsense." It wasn't that picking players from Riverview, our church school, was hard. No, the "nonsense" was having to make sure the kids actually came to rehearsals, wore what they were supposed to wear, and didn't flub their very few lines. While her cantata might have yielded the occasional squeaky note, and its pace may have sagged abominably more than once, she still had full control over the grown-ups and knew what to expect. With kids, however, all bets were off: someone was sure to giggle, a shepherd might faint, and she never knew when an angel might slip away to the outhouse attached to the church for a bathroom break. It simply wasn't worth it.

The year I was nine was only the second time in my life she had mustered the fortitude to add the pageant piece to her cantata. The previous time, the young players had acted out the story during the matching musical numbers. It worked like this: when Eldon Lee called out, "Make haste in the desert, a highway to our God," for instance, three bathrobe-wearing Magi hurried up the aisle. Unfortunately, Grammy found the whole live-action business so distracting from the choir's carefully rehearsed numbers that she vowed never to do it that way again. This time, the cantata would be completed before the pageant portion started, and the nativity scene would instead be accompanied by the junior choir singing traditional carols.

I was dying for a part. There was no chance of Grammy ever spicing up the cantata enough to include me playing Scrooge—his was a worldly story, after all—so my only chance for a big number was to get a role in the pageant. With luck, I would get cast as a wise man, though Grammy said she thought I was too young. I would've even settled for an angel, though Grammy thought that I was too male (if just barely . . .). I knew for sure I didn't want to be Joseph, who would have to just stand there mute the whole time, and Grammy said there wasn't really a little drummer boy in the true story, so I couldn't be that either.

She nearly cast a brother and sister, Mark and Kimi, as Mary and Joseph, but my brother and I reacted so negatively—Ew! No one marries his sister!—that she reconsidered, instead shuffling Mark into one of the wise men roles. The other two slots were given to Ignacio and—oh happy day!—me. Yes, I would be the third wise man, doomed to bring up the rear, but that still meant I got to sing a solo verse myself, as well as wear a veil-draped crown. That vision made up for the fact that Mark and I were like oil and water: he was tall, thin and sporty, and I was short, chubby, and bookish. Mark never seemed the brightest bulb on the tree, but he could nonetheless discern exactly which insults would make me burn. He first tormented me by calling me a girl every time I played tetherball or four square, but then he switched gears and settled on the nickname he would call me for years: Porker.

Bullies are brilliant. They can reduce a weaker kid into a completely defined package with a single word or phrase. "Porker" cemented my identity as the fat kid. Granted, I *was* the fat kid, but I had never realized that other people noticed or cared until I had a nickname to live up to. The first time he said it, I was red with anger.

"Don't call me Porker!"

His reply: "Okay, Porker."

There was to be no let up, and I knew it. It didn't matter that no one else ever used the nickname except, occasionally, one of his buddies. "Porker" continually stunk up the air every time I was around Mark, which just meant that I chose not to be around him often. Now, Grammy had thrown us together. And yet, I secretly relished the opportunity to be on a team of kings with Mark. Why? Because I could sing better. All those hours imitating Dolly Parton and Marty Robbins had made my young voice smooth and sweet. Mark could sing, but his voice was a little more nasal, and there was nothing especially lyrical about it. Let Mark be first king, I thought. I'd be the one whose solo everyone remembered.

On Christmas morning, we gathered in our living room a half-hour before the church service was to start. We lived directly across the street from the church, which was convenient for many reasons, not the least of which being that we could run home to use the bathroom, instead of using the church's century-old two-seater outhouse. On this day, our proximity to the church meant that the kids in the pageant could get dressed and stay out of sight nearby until needed. Our house was abuzz with activity: there were garland-trimmed angel wings to tie on, pillow cases to transform into shepherd-wear, and Magi to make royal.

It had been decided that, instead of wearing bathrobes, we would wear baptismal robes that year as they were more regal looking. I was thrilled at how the hem of my black gown dragged along the floor like the train on a wedding dress. The crowns, however, presented a momentary crisis: only two of the stiff cardboard miters still had their flowing silk scarves stapled on. I'm not sure who decided that Magi should so resemble pastel versions of Greek Orthodox priests, but it was a look I thought was just marvelous—and I was afraid that I would get the plain crown because of my third-wise-man status. I was already contemplating rooting through Grammy's dresser for the sheer pink scarf that she wore whenever she needed to protect a fresh set of big roller curls, but then Mark grabbed the one unadorned crown, happily crowing, "You're a girl, Porker, so you have to take one with a scarf." He said this like I was somehow losing out and not instantly improving the fabulousness of my costume. My brother did not seem to like the implications of this statement at all, seeing as he too had one of the crowns Mark had just gendered, but Ignacio didn't dare remove the drapery and risk Grammy's wrath.

The gifts of frankincense, myrrh, and gold were to be represented by a music box, a glass perfume bottle, and a yellow metal compact, which Grammy clearly didn't get from an Adventist, who would have no use for the blue and teal eye shadow which remained inside. I wanted the "incense" because that meant I would get to carry the pretty music box, which was decorated with an intricate embossed filigree. What I did not want was the compact, which was just plain ugly and stupid—no one would believe that old thing was a bar of gold. To my delight, that was the gift Mark got since the gold verse was the first solo in the carol. When Grammy gave Ignacio the music box, I decided on the spot that incense was the wrong gift for me anyway; myrrh was a perfume and I *liked* perfume, so I gladly accepted the red glass bottle she handed me. Then, newly inspired, I asked Grammy if we could fill it with some of Mom's "White Shoulders" eau de cologne, but Grammy said it was a nativity scene and the only smell in the real manger was something nobody wanted to bottle.

We were told not to head over to the church until fifteen minutes after the cantata started, as it always did, precisely at 11 AM. Even then, we were to hang out in the foyer until the appropriate moment, making sure that our appearance wouldn't distract anyone in the audience from focusing on the choir. Tiptoeing as much as elementary schoolchildren could, we entered the foyer just about the time my mother, Aunt Marion, and our friend June began my favorite song in the show. "Hark! What mean those holy voices," they crooned, "sweetly sounding through the skies?" Mark started to whisper something, and I shushed him because I thought this trio made just about the sweetest harmony on earth; plus, they were coming to the good part, a glorious peak that all three women had to take a breath for. I didn't want the spell to be broken, especially by Mark.

Nine songs later, by the time the cantata ended, I was more than ready to make an entrance worthy of a king. First, though, I had to wait for Mary and Joseph to get up the aisle to put Baby Jesus away in His manger. Then, the angels had to hark their heralds. After that, the shepherds had to lay in their fields for the first Noel. Finally, it was time for my—I mean, our—entrance. "We three Kings of Orient are," we sang in high unison, a little like the Jackson Five but without soul, as we stepped into the sanctuary. As we passed the tape recorder Grampy had set up in a back row to record the pageant, I made sure to sing especially loudly so my debut would be captured for posterity.

"Born a king on Bethlehem's plain," Mark began shakily. I felt a little pity for him, poor guy standing there with a cheap yellow compact in hand, his crown completely underdressed for the occasion, and his voice wavering with nerves. After the chorus, Ignacio acquitted himself much better, getting up over the hurdle of the high note on "voices raising," even though his own voice was starting to lower. One more chorus, and it would be my moment in the sun.

The lyrics for my verse were perfect for a little drama queen in the making:

Myrrh is mine
its bitter perfume
breathes a life of gathering gloom
sorrowing, sighing, bleeding, dying,
sealed in the stone cold tomb.

I suppose those lines are a wee bit dark for a festive occasion, but they were all the better for a would-be performer to emote. Raising my red vial aloft, I launched into the most passionate rendition possible, but my voice wasn't cooperating. My throat felt tight, and my hands began to shake. I was somewhere between bleeding and dying when the words dropped out completely. There was a croak, followed by dead air, as I panicked and realized that I wasn't making any sound. The pianist kept going, but I managed only to catch up in the last phrase, gargling out a deeply tortured version of "stone cold tomb."

Mark and Ignacio didn't dare even glance at me as the junior choir moved right on to the final chorus. But Grammy fixed me with a look that could have wrinkled granite. I knew I had to stand there like a man and literally face the music, showing as much dignity as I could in the face of my abysmal failure. I did what any aspiring professional would: I fled. Leaving two stunned kings in my wake, I raced down the aisle, now truly aflutter, face as red as the bottle in my sweaty hand. Tears of anger filled my eyes as I hurried home, berating myself. Instead of dazzling the church with my grand performance, I had given Mark the victory. Worse, I had become that annual kid who caused Grammy to reconsider ever doing a pageant again.

And yet, that is a Christmas I remember with some fondness. For that night, after so much delay, we opened our presents, and I learned that sometimes you really do get what you want. Inside a shoebox, beneath a layer of tissue paper, I found a pair of white leather figure skates that just begged for ice-dancing routines and sequined costumes. Unlike the year of the doll, no one seemed to want me to give back my present, and Grammy, my morning performance now history, was in fine spirits as I gushed with happiness over the gift. Ignacio, sad to say, would not look back on that evening with similar joy. For he, too, had gotten a pair of white figure skates, not at all what he had in mind. I don't know how the grown-ups had so obviously missed the gender distinctions that all the kids were focused on, and I feel badly for Ignacio in retrospect, having the sweater-vest Christmas followed up by the girly-skates Christmas. But for me, this gift completely erased the sting of "Porker" and the shame of fleeing my own debut.

I held the skates to my chest the way a new Miss America clutches her roses: with joy and relief and visions of the glorious days ahead.

7

Ambrosia

My grandmother's photo albums were the antithesis of her house; rooms she kept neat as a pin, but her albums were a jumble of snapshots organized by whim and ease, if it all. A black-and-white photo of Grampy in a swimsuit in the 1940s might very well be taped down next to a color Polaroid of my brother and me dressed in our minutemen outfits for a bicentennial parade. Our school photos each got a whole page, but even they were out of order, so we got older for several pages in a row, then suddenly regressed.

Beyond organization, the primary things missing from Grammy's albums were Christmas pictures. For a woman who never failed to get a good snapshot of the aftermath of a snowstorm and who had immortalized several not-especially-impressive African violets on film, it was an unpredictable glitch that she kept no yuletide photos at all, aside from three color shots of the very first Christmas my brother and I lived in her house.

In 1977, however, we had a stack of Christmas party photos to choose from. They were all taken from the same vantage point beyond the far end of the holiday dinner table at my Aunt Jean and Uncle Fred's house and thus looked nearly identical. Yet I loved them for their rarity—not just because they were Christmas pictures but because they captured so much of our family together. These snapshots owed their existence to the fact that Mom had a new Kodak Instamatic camera with a built-in flash. Longer than a pack of cigarettes and only slightly thicker, it was a tiny piece of equipment, but it was big enough for her to hide behind. Behind that camera, Mom—never a big talker—found a buffer from the endless chatter.

Aunt Jean and Uncle Fred lived just up the street from us, but their house was worlds away on every level. While our house was a two-hundred-year-old colonial with no heat on the top floor, theirs was a twentieth-century raised ranch with sliding doors leading to a deck upstairs and a finished basement below. I was fascinated by the exotic contents of the house, like a television the size of a dishwasher, ashtrays that appeared to be more than just decorative, and actual alcohol, unlike in our house where no one smoked or drank.

Grammy was not crazy about certain elements of her eldest daughter's lifestyle, but she was nonetheless proud of Jean, who had bravely endured the death of her first husband in his twenties; she was a widowed mother of three when she married Fred, with whom she had one more child. While Grampy and Grammy were blue collar, both working in shoe shops, Jean and Fred were solidly middle class. They owned a jewelry store in Waterville, which made them almost city folk. Even teenage Adrienne, their one child remaining at home, seemed otherworldly to Ignacio and me: She had black-light posters, rock albums, and an attitude, all of which made me feel like the country cousin, even though I lived a two-minute walk from her house.

That year, Jean and Fred hosted a Christmas party in their "finished" basement, the crown jewel of which was Fred's bar. Grammy hated even to look at the thing, seeing as its entire purpose was the serving up of one shot of sin after another, but we kids found it dazzling. The bar had a waist-high counter that doubled as a stereo, and when music was playing, the front lit up in a variety of colors that pulsed with the beat. In front of the bar, padded stools swiveled perfectly, and behind it were shelves lined with beer steins, hard liquor, and cocktail glasses. It was like a groovy pub with Fred as the mix-master, not that I knew exactly what he was mixing.

Besides, I preferred Aunt Jean's specialty: ambrosia. I only had this confection of whipped cream, coconut, mandarin oranges, and pineapple at Jean's house, and only then at the holidays, and its rarity made it seem so special that I couldn't get enough of the stuff. Grammy used some of the same ingredients in her Jell-O-mold desserts from time to time, but those dishes were always brightly colored with the aid of strawberry or lime gelatin mix. Aunt Jean's dessert was white, like mounds of snow, and it seemed to me the very essence of winter in a Chinette bowl. When Christmas dinner was ready that year, I offered to carry the ambrosia down the stairs, and I held it carefully like the treasure it was.

The basement was abuzz, crowded with more than just the occupants of our two houses. Adrienne's older sister Glenice had come up from Massachusetts with her husband, Dave, a rising insurance salesman. And Uncle Ronald, the only one of Grammy's boys who lived nearby, was there with his cheery chatterbox of a wife, Aunt Marie. That brought the total to a dozen for dinner, which meant that there wasn't space enough at the table for all the kids—and yet, there was room for me.

I was such a determined little suck-up. I found grown-up conversations so enticing that I had to be a part of them. I made sure to listen attentively to every story, laugh at every joke I didn't understand, and even add to the conversation, whether or not my contributions made any sense. While Adrienne and Ignacio seemed plenty happy just to roll their eyes at the adults, I longed for the grown-ups to find me charming, amusing, and smart. I wanted them to like me—no, I wanted them to like me *best*. Though I may have been included at the table because Adrienne and Ignacio could not have cared less where they ate, I was sure I had gotten a seat because everyone could see how much I would add to the proceedings. Ambrosia salad before me and adults on all sides, I reveled in the glory of my esteemed position.

When Mom developed the party pictures a week later, I had incontrovertible evidence that I'd had exactly the Christmas I wanted. Still, at a glance the photos weren't all that impressive; in not a single shot does everyone look at the camera all at once. We appear to be just another family caught with our mouths full in the middle of a holiday dinner. But, then again, what family really is "just another family"? The dramas that play out between people who love each other, the histories between the holidays, are specific. And when I revisited these photos years later, I realized the air that night had been full not only of cheery tunes blasting from a pulsing light-up bar, but thick, too, with grudges, hopes, sadness, and reconciliation. Mom never intended to capture those things at all, yet she had.

Standing behind the dinner table in my favorite photo of that night, Uncle Fred appears in motion, his hand on his chest as if graciously asking our pardon. A survivor of Pearl Harbor and a host of battles in the South Pacific, he typically had little patience for kids who ran around slamming doors and making other sudden noises. But that Christmas Fred had gotten Ignacio a BB gun, a gift that must have seemed like a no-brainer to a military man like Fred, and he'd been unpleasantly surprised to find himself facing Grammy's fury. She thought the present was too violent; he thought she should keep her opinions to herself.

Closest to Fred are Dave and Glenice, sitting with their shoulders touching, though Dave is leaning forward to be better seen. As a child, I saw them in a golden light, the sophisticated visitors from the cosmopolitan land of Massachusetts. Glenice was a high school teacher, and Dave was running for local city office. Grammy and Grampy never quite settled on how they felt about him, with his lascivious jokes and alcohol ever in hand; I thought he was akin to a celebrity and was thrilled when he gave me a campaign button with his name on it. But his glow was already on the brink of fading as an unseemly personal transgression would cost him everything—political career and marriage—soon enough.

Next to Glenice sits Aunt Jean. The tight expression on her unsmiling face reflects an absence that she no doubt was feeling keenly that day. Her only son had just been convicted of murder in the first degree, sentenced to life in prison for the death of his partner in a detective agency. The prevailing theory in our household was that a woman roundly regarded by the family as a temptress had killed the partner and pinned everything on Jean's son. But the jury didn't know him or her, and nobody asked us our opinions, so he was sent away for ninety-nine years without a chance of parole. Even as we praised her ambrosia and avoided talking about the missing son, Aunt Jean was off in another world. Far from her son and helpless to aid him, it must've been everything she could do to swallow.

Next to her, Grampy raises his fork to his mouth for a bite of pie. He and Grammy sit kitty-corner from each other, not side by side. He looks tense and grumpy, and for good reason. His inner Romeo had gotten him into trouble again. He simply could not seem to keep his hands to himself when hugging the women at church, dear friends who were startled when a hug became an embrace of another sort. When a particular set of old friends separated, Grampy had written a letter to the newly alone wife to suggest methods of consolation that shocked her and, in turn, made Grammy so furious she could barely stand to share a room with him. Married fifty-one years that Christmas, he was in the doghouse again, which no one was supposed to bring up and we kids weren't supposed to know (but did).

Across from Grampy sits Uncle Ronald, who resembles Grampy in surface ways. Both sport widow's peaks, sour looks, and plaid pants. Yet Ronald seemed ever above the fray. He didn't ask about family gossip, didn't get caught up in the drama. The one point of contention was unspoken: we saw his family less often than we saw Jean's because Marie, barely visible in the photo, was hard-core Catholic and didn't want to expose her children to Grammy's religion, which she saw as a little crazy. This, of course, irked Grammy, who was used to being the one who feared the contaminating effects of unbelievers.

On the other side of Marie, I lean into the picture to make sure I'm noticed. I'm in my favorite shirt, a busy little number rife with red and blue horizontal stripes, topped by a thick, round collar. It was as close as I could come to dressing like a cast member from my very favorite television show, *Zoom,* but it makes me look dangerously like Ernie from *Sesame Street.* I'm also sporting a new haircut from Roy's barber shop, where I had convinced the kindly barber that I wanted my dark hair cut all one length without a part, which I thought made me look kind of like Dorothy Hamill, at least as much as an overweight ten-year-old boy could. That was the most outward sign of my inner desire to be more of a "girly boy" than I knew my family would like.

Behind me in the photo, Adrienne slouches on a barstool against the wall, wearing her coolest disaffected look. She radiates lack of interest. Part of Adrienne's allure for me as a child was that she was everything I was not: world-weary, jaded, and willing to sass back. These traits made her seem goddesslike to me, but they weren't exactly evidence of a happy time for her, and they hardly ingratiated her with her parents, who put her in a "girl's school" for a while to avoid fights at home. What neither they nor I knew then was that Adrienne felt about girls the way I felt about boys.

My brother sits next to Adrienne on a barstool, a proximity that has liberated him. Forget any pretense of being well behaved: he is sticking out his tongue and looks dangerously close to flipping the bird. He had plenty to be mad about, including the unfortunate distinction of having the single most ethnic name in our entire überwhite town. I had gotten off easy with the more ecumenical name of David, while he was saddled with Ignacio, a name deemed unpronounceable by his little league teammates (who called him "Mac"), his best friends (who called him "Nash"), and even by one of his teachers (who called him "egghead," which says less about Ignacio's ethnicity and more about the man's professionalism). Sick of being seen as both bad seed and half-breed, he finally had something to celebrate that holiday: the BB gun from Uncle Fred. Who cared how Grammy felt about it. At last, *somebody* understood him.

Grammy, the centrifugal force of the family, holds center court in the photo. Yet the chinks in her armor are visible here. Her strong chin rests in one hand, and the look on her face is one of weary indulgence. She does not want to smile for any more pictures, and she's tired as the day is long. The night before, when Mom was hours late coming home, we waited nervously by the blinking lights of our Christmas tree, tensed for the sound of her car or the ringing of the phone. Grammy was sure something bad had happened—and she was right. Mom had flipped her Rambler into a gully on the road to Waterville and would stay there trapped in the dark for almost two hours before anyone noticed. The weight of that near loss merely added to Grammy's fatigue: Just when she was supposed to be relaxing in her golden years of retirement, she found herself sharing her house with an out-of-work daughter and two young boys who worked her nerves nearly as badly as Grampy did.

Yet for all its hidden secrets and implied dramas, the photo didn't lie about Christmas 1977's being a happy holiday. Like any family portrait, it simply revealed a different kind of truth for each viewer. It would be many years before I would understand the complicated meanings embedded in this snapshot, but for me as a child, the story it told was absolutely joyful. Holding it in my hand, I could feel the specific magic of the party: the honeyed tone of Bing Crosby's voice on the stereo, the colors blinking red and green in the glowing bar, the sound of people I loved laughing and talking all around me. What a Christmas.

What an ambrosia.

8

The Shoestring
Santa Blues

Socks. No other word from my childhood Christmases so instantly raises my hackles, even though I am now supposed to be a mature adult. By the time I was eleven, a new pattern had been set: under the tree, my brother and I could each expect only two presents, one of which was a two-pack of white tube socks. This was as true for Mom as for us boys, but that didn't lessen the sting.

Even as a child I knew—or, to be clear, I had been told—the reasoning behind this purchase. First off, with my family now living on social security and food stamps, gifts had to be practical. Besides that, there were millions of children around the world who would be getting no presents at all and who would have been thrilled to unwrap the very same present I sighed at unhappily like an ingrate. The topper was the reminder that presents were not *the reason for the season* anyway. That very pointed comment was supposed to tap into all my youthful religious guilt, but it didn't. With each yuletide, the ritual of tearing the previous year's carefully recycled wrapping paper off these predictably mundane bundles grew more joyless.

I decided to do something about it. It was up to me to set a good gift-giving example to teach Grammy, the admitted giver of socks, that it was possible to give decent presents while still sticking to a budget.

My plan was simple: I would be a living role model of festive frugality, and Grammy would be so impressed that she would follow suit out of inspiration or shame or both. To make this happen, I would have to use up the small amount of cash I kept on hand. My new housecleaning gig for Aunt Jean and Uncle Fred was my one reliable source of income. For $2.50 a week, I vacuumed, cleaned the shower, and Windexed every mirror in the house.

A couple of months on my new job had earned me $17.50, a sum that had decreased because I was expected to give my church both a tithe of 10 percent (lopping $1.75 off the top) and an "offering" of 5 percent (another 88 cents gone). That left $14.87, which I had lessened further by indulging in the *Grease* issue of *Cracked* magazine, which I found hilarious and Mom let me buy, even though Grammy called it "filth." With roughly $14 still in hand, I had all the resources I would be able to muster to shop for my entire list. Therein lay a small problem: there were thirty-six names on that list.

Obviously, I needed something for my immediate family members, and certainly I had to include my new employers, seeing as they had made my bounty possible, but there were also classmates and teachers to consider, and that was just the beginning. There were the Gallants, whose own grandchildren lived far away and who traded off with my grandparents every so often: Grampy and Grammy would get a quiet house for the afternoon, and the Gallants would get two proxy grandsons to take on excursions to fish hatcheries and salmon locks. I also wanted to get something for my favorite neighbor, Emma McKenney, who lived across the way in a trailer full of puppies and cigarette smoke; we watched TV together, and she delighted me with a cackling laugh like nothing I ever heard at home.

I needed something, too, for Old Mrs. Stanley, the town librarian, who kindly let me sit in the storage room sifting through years-old *People* magazines. In a dusty room lit brightly by an ancient window, I could sort through the glossy stacks, hunting without embarrassment for issues about my icons: Cher, Carol Burnett, Laverne and Shirley, and Watergate figure Martha Mitchell, whose hair was big but whose mouth was even bigger. It was also in these stacks that I could most openly nourish celebrity crushes, soaking in tales of David Bowie and Warren Beatty. Mrs. Stanley clearly deserved a present for making it possible. Indeed, the world seemed full of people needing gifts, and I determined that I was just the boy to fill this need.

"Can someone take me to Skowhegan?" I asked one December Sunday morning. This was a somewhat insincere request as the only person in the kitchen was Grammy, who was unlikely to grant it.

She could read my tone and knew something was up. Pausing over a mixing bowl of fruitcake batter, she took the bait. "What foolishness are you getting up to now?"

"I just need to do my Christmas shopping," I said as innocently as I could. "I have thirty-six people to buy presents for, and I need to make sure they *all* get something they'll *like!*"

Grammy just made a "tsking" sound and went back to mixing her famous concoction. I say famous because all the grown-ups in our extended family and a slew of friends from church expected a loaf of the sticky brown horror every year. To my disbelief, they even seemed to like it, thanking her profusely and taking the leaden prize home with them where I couldn't help but wonder if it became a doorstop or something to threaten their children with: "You be good, or Daddy's getting out the fruitcake!"

I did not yet know that fruitcake is almost always terrible, that fruitcake jokes are a staple of holiday humor, and that an urban legend suggests that the number of loaves in existence is finite, the same ones getting passed unopened from victim to victim each year. I only knew that Grammy, who made dreamworthy fudge and unsurpassed pumpkin pie, somehow blew it when it came to this stuff. I dreaded being served a gummy slice, with its shudder-making candied fruit in a shade of chemical green seen in no natural thing on earth.

She noticed I was still standing there. "Ask your Mom," she said. "I have to make fruitcake."

"You don't *have* to make it," I said, perhaps indiscreetly.

"You don't *have* to stand there." I hated to admit it, but she did a pretty good imitation of me.

Having received the expected response from Grammy, I sought out Mom, who was watching a black-and-white movie on TV. There were two reasons I asked her for a ride to Skowhegan instead of to Waterville, where the grown-ups did their Christmas shopping: there was no chance Mom could be talked into going to the city on a whim, and beyond that, I assumed that I couldn't afford city prices for my presents anyway. If she took me to the smaller, nearer town of Skowhegan, I could head straight for the promised land of affordable shopping, LaVerdiere's Super Drug Store. If there was ever a place to get more than thirty gifts for under fifteen bucks, that was it. Happily, Mom agreed to indulge me.

Note that LaVerdiere's was no mere drugstore—it was a *super* drugstore. This was not false advertising. Long before Wal-Mart, LaVerdiere's was playing the everything-in-one-place game—just in a very small place. You could fill a prescription for antibiotics, pick up a copy of *LIFE* magazine, refresh your supply of Bag

Balm, buy a gift set of Jean Naté cologne, grab a handful of Slim Jims, try on a pair of Isotoner gloves, and find a Waylon Jennings LP all in one stop. The aisles were narrow because the merchandise leaned in on all sides, and it was easy to hide out of sight if, for instance, you wanted privacy as you took a quick peek at *Tiger Beat.* I knew that if my quest was to be completed, I had to begin here.

I saw shiny plastic eggs stuffed with pantyhose and was tempted to turn the tables on Grammy, stocking for stocking, but knew this gift would be too naked a rebuttal. Grampy's gift was easier: a three-pack of paintbrushes, which he could use in completing the Paint By Numbers landscapes that consumed a good part of his day. Ignacio would get a pack of Monster Cards, each card depicting a horrible creature from the movies, accompanied by that stale pink gum that always reminded me of a tongue depressor. Then I stumbled on a holiday stickpin, which I figured Grammy might actually use since she occasionally dressed up her good church suit with a brooch. I still had $12 left, but I knew that for nonfamily members, I was going to have to speed up my process, or I'd never be finished before Mom grew tired of waiting for me.

I turned down the aisle of Christmas supplies and found myself in a wonderland of shopping. The boxed ornament sets leapt out at me here: I could get six, eight, even twelve gifts at once for only a few dollars.

This was perfect, I thought, because *everyone* likes Christmas, right? I just needed to give people the ornaments they'd most appreciate. I snagged a mixed set of twelve wooden animals, another of eight colorful bulbs. The third box was a variety pack of a dozen reindeer, angels, snowmen, and wee carolers. Just like that, I had thirty-five of my thirty-six presents in hand a mere hour after announcing my plan to Grammy. I paid for my loot and hurried triumphantly out to the parking lot where Mom was warming up the car. Already sure that I was the most efficient of Santas, I made the thrilling discovery that I still had three precious dollars left in my wallet.

That meant I could get something really good for Mom that I couldn't find in LaVerdiere's. With my father distant and Grammy so mercurial, I felt bonded with my mother and very protective. I hated it when she was depressed and loved it when she was happy, and I thought it was my job to keep her that way. I knew exactly what I wanted. An Avon Lady had been at my great aunt Marion's house many months before, and I had seen there the absolute epitome of glamour: a bell-shaped crystal decanter filled with pink "Roses, Roses" perfume. If it was under $3, I would get it for Mom, and she was sure to just swoon.

It took a day or two for Aunt Marion to get me the number for the Avon Lady, who seemed surprised to receive a phone call at home from an eleven-year-old boy customer, especially one with such a specific request. She warned me that products were seasonal and that the bell in question was really *last* year's bell; the new bell was emerald green and just as good, she said, but she could tell by the way I recoiled—um, roses aren't *green*—that it was the pink bell or nothing. She said she'd see what she could do.

To pass the following days while I waited for her word, I wrapped thirty-five individual presents. Ignacio's, Grammy's, and Grampy's all looked pretty small, but I tried to perch these gifts on others under the tree to increase their stature. Once removed from their cartons, the other thirty-two multipack presents were not only small but awkwardly shaped for wrapping, and I was sure that at least one of the light glass bulbs would implode before they were all delivered, thus killing my count. Eager to have the gifts safely out of my hands a full two weeks before Christmas, I started visiting neighbors late that same afternoon, with many of them evincing clear surprise, seeing as we'd never exchanged gifts before. I took the remainder of my bundles to school the next day, then finished up with a visit to the library where Mrs. Stanley accepted her present with an air of pleased puzzlement.

It was getting dark when I finally got home. Grammy wanted to know where I'd been. This was my chance to say that I had just finished delivering all the presents I had bought with my humble savings. I made a big show of expressing how proud I was to give *good* gifts and how *happy* people were that I had thought of them. Grammy shrugged.

"Well, good for you, but you missed a phone call."

The Avon Lady had rung to say she had found last year's bell. I had a momentary panic—had Mom heard this call?—but Grammy told me she'd figured it was a surprise and hadn't said anything to Mom. When I spoke to the Avon Lady that night, she told me I could pick up the bell at Marion's house and, yes, it was under $3, which I could leave with my aunt.

I had done it. And I had no intention of being shy about my grand achievement. In the days before Christmas, I bragged endlessly about my vigilance and cleverness. I should have just gotten a T-shirt bearing the slogan "36-for-14!" and given everyone's ears a rest. But I was a typical missionary boy: I needed to spread the good word to ensure my example was followed.

I got socks.

I stewed all Christmas morning, sure of the wrongness of what had just happened. I wanted to pick a fight. When I found Grammy in the kitchen, slicing herself a hunk of the last dreaded loaf, I chose the risky and unusual tack of speaking to her in overtly sarcastic tones. "Is that more of your little fruitcake?"

She didn't miss a beat. "Nope. *You're* my little fruit-cake."

Her retort surprised me so much I almost laughed out loud, but I didn't; there was no way on earth I would've let her see me smile.

That night, by the time we headed up the street to Aunt Jean and Uncle Fred's house for our Christmas visit, my sourness was already lifting, as I am constitutionally incapable of maintaining a bad mood for too long. Grammy wore her stickpin, even though she wasn't in her church suit, which made me feel a little better. Mom told everyone about her bell, which I had to agree was pretty spectacular in its own faux-crystal way. And Jean made sure to point out the place on their tree where the reindeer ornament I'd gotten them was hanging. It was the first time I realized that, as much as I hated getting socks, I loved giving presents. My quest, despite not having its intended effect, had been worth it.

And then the universe itself gave *me* a gift, a memory that outshines all others from that year. Grampy and Grammy drove home from Jean and Fred's, with Ignacio hitching a ride in the car to keep out of the snow that had been falling steadily all evening. But Mom and I decided to walk back down the street. The world's usual murmur was muffled by the new snow, and there were no plows in sight, nor any other traffic. At the far end of our street, we could see the only stoplight in town blinking red, as it always did. We walked arm in arm, taking careful steps so that we wouldn't slip on patches of ice beneath the white powder. It was so quiet, so truly still, that I was sure I could hear the pit-pit touchdown of snowflakes, and even the blink of the stoplight seemed audible, a faint heartbeat.

It made me think of a Robert Frost poem we had just learned in school in which the writer can hear the sound of "easy wind and downy flake." When I told Mom I was thinking of a poem, she surprised me by saying she could guess which one. Despite the fact that my mother had also attended school in Norridgewock and had even had the same elementary and junior high school teachers as I did, it had never occurred to me that she might have learned this poem herself. (In those days, I was always astounded—and sometimes a little dismayed—when a grown-up actually knew something interesting.) "Whose woods these are," she began, to my great delight, and I joined her in reciting the poem aloud as we walked.

Arm in arm with my mother, leaning homeward, it didn't seem such a failed Christmas after all. There was still plenty of time for me to spread the gospel of shoestring gift giving in the years ahead. We had miles to go before any of us slept. And new socks to keep our feet warm for the journey.

9

Tree Envy

B lame it on the Daughters of the American Revolution, but I had a wicked case of tree envy.

I had always loved our Christmas tree, its variety-pack bulbs making it glow like a carnival ride, while a hodgepodge of ornaments testified to the haphazard evolution of my family's aesthetics. The red Grampy and Grammy mice held places of honor as they had since the 1950s and were joined by 1960s-era plastic diamonds filled with frosted pipe cleaner "trees," corn-husk angels (part of the colonial craze from the country's bicentennial in 1976), and several adorable clothespin reindeer (from the White Elephant Sale at church).

At twelve, I was too old just to lie on the floor and gaze up at the tree in dreamy adoration as I had many holidays in a row. But I still looked forward to getting the tree up every year, which marked the official beginning of the Christmas season (as opposed to the unofficial beginning, when the LaVerdiere's specialty goods aisle swapped out its plastic pumpkins for plastic snowmen). Just one year before, Grammy had agreed to let me help out in a task that had always been hers alone: decorating the tree. It was surprising that she welcomed my participation because the truth is that we were not exactly the most harmonious of teams. Grammy and I could fight about anything, even when we were in basic agreement.

The previous Christmas, our first collaboration on the tree, things had started out smoothly enough. I figured Grammy knew what she was doing, so I followed her lead. Everything stayed peaceable until we got to the candy canes. She had bought a bag of loose red-and-white canes, which she hung directly on the tree because she considered them ornaments. I, however, saw them as both decoration *and* snack and complained that an unwrapped candy cane would come into contact with the sticky pitch of a fir bough, rendering it not just gross but inedible. I pointed out that there were individually wrapped candy canes at the drugstore that she could hang on the tree instead—far more sanitary and thus better suited to consumption.

She promptly informed me that if I wanted to go buy those candy canes, I was welcome to; otherwise, she was hanging up the ones from the bag she'd already opened, and I could like it or lump it. She was pretty convinced that her young grandson was not going to waste his meager earnings to win this argument, and she was right. Her canes went up, and I made a pouty show of not eating any; my resolve lasted for an entire day before I broke down and took one off the tree to suck on, ignoring both the piney aftertaste and Grammy's triumphant amusement at my weak will.

When it came time to decorate for the second year, she might have expected that I would be similarly compliant. But Grammy had not seen what I had: the stunning masterpiece of holiday wonder that graced the very large living room in the home of one of the local Daughters of the American Revolution. The women of the DAR sponsored essay contests, held charity events, and planted flags on the oldest gravestones in town. Grammy knew one of these white-haired matrons and had arranged for my brother and me to sing at her functions several times over the previous years. I'd been summoned to her house that winter to receive, as a thank you, a keepsake wallet housing the newly minted Susan B. Anthony dollar coins. Though I thanked DAR Lady politely, I wasn't impressed by the coins, which looked like quarters with an unhappy woman on them. I reserved my real enthusiasm for the tree.

In an enormous parlor, a thickly symmetrical cone of tree perfection sloped upward from the floor to within an inch or two of the high ceiling. At home, our fir not only never approached the ceiling but rarely reached six feet. This was because, at 5'8", my fourteen-year-old brother was the tallest resident of our house by a good three inches. Grammy, just over five feet, was shortest, and she had no interest in climbing a ladder to hang decorations. The result was that even our nicest tree was just slightly taller than we were, and only a hobbit would've had trouble crowning it with a plastic angel.

Already impressed by the stature of DAR Lady's tree, I was further wowed by the precision of its ornamentation. The ornaments, including real glass ones, were all discreet in size and placed with a scrupulous eye for balance. It was like a grid that mapped out holiday flawlessness; if there was a small, shiny orb in the top left section of the tree, a similar ball appeared in the lower right, and so on and so forth in three dimensions until the ornaments were as organically integrated into the whole as the limbs.

Then there was the matter of tinsel. We were definitely tinsel people and used the stuff liberally, without any special subtlety. But DAR Lady showed me a whole new way of thinking about it. It seemed, impossibly, as if her tinsel strands had been individually placed for maximum shimmering potential. There were no handfuls, no clusters, just thousands of ethereal foil ribbons placed as particularly as the ornaments. The tree seemed an unbroken sheet of silver that rippled softly with any movement of air. How on earth had she pulled it off?

My hostess was proud of her handiwork. "I hang every piece of tinsel one strand at a time. It takes forever, but I do think it glorifies the tree. Don't you?" I was in awe of her devotion. I thought of how my family blindly tossed clumps of tinsel at our little tree, and I felt ashamed, suddenly sure that we were insulting the poor fir whose life had been ended solely for our merriment.

The more I inspected this Apex of Treedom, the more negative comparisons I made to our tree at home. For one thing, there wasn't a single strand of garland on her tree, but we were as heavy-handed with garland as we were with tinsel. We used skinny burgundy garland, fat blue-green garland, and a few lengths of ratty gold garland, recycled from many Christmases past. The strands crisscrossed each other until they ran out, with the gold garland not quite making it halfway up the tree. No such gaudy trappings marred the DAR Lady's creation.

The kicker was her lights. They were all white. I had never imagined such a thing. Our tree was festooned with hot-to-the-touch colored bulbs the size of thumbs. Some of the older ones appeared to have their colors painted on, while the more recent ones were translucent; this combination of clear and opaque bulbs was a likable optical illusion, where some branches appeared closer or further away than they actually were. The vast majority of our bulbs came in straight-ahead shades of blue, red, green, yellow, and orange, though one in every six was milk white. I had previously seen this colorless minority as the worst of the lot: boring, no-personality bulbs that interrupted the rainbow splendor of the rest of the tree. But I had never seen white lights quite like the ones on DAR Lady's tree. Here were translucent miniature bulbs in the shape of candle tips, tiny pinpoints twinkling among fir boughs like countless stars in an evergreen sky. This was so-phistication! This was glamour! This was a big fight with Grammy waiting to happen.

Having learned the lesson of the candy canes the year before, I armed myself in advance this time. On a re-cent outing to LaVerdiere's, I had found two strings of white lights that I could afford and a fresh box of tin-sel, sure that ours, which we reused every year, would be a wrinkled mess that would compromise my vision of perfection. I said nothing of my purchases until the Sunday afternoon Grampy made his annual trip to the tree farm run by the local chief of police, then re-turned with a fine balsam fir, which he hauled into the living room and set up in our dented metal tree stand.

As Grammy opened the cardboard chests in which our Christmas ornaments were stored, I put a few holi-day LPs on the record player to set the mood. I kept my back to her, fiddling with the arm of the record player as I said I had some new ideas for the tree. Grammy was good, *really* good, at arguments, so she simply didn't re-spond; she waited me out till I had to turn around and look her in the eye to explain my big vision. We both knew her silence for the warning it was.

I produced my strings of white lights and said I thought they were actually prettier than all the colored bulbs. I ventured that having now seen the DAR Lady's classy decorations, I was worried that maybe our bright bulbs came off as a little tacky. Grammy asked what made me so sure that the DAR Lady qualified as classy, and before I could answer that, she asked me if I knew that "tacky" was an insult. I switched gears, saying I also thought the white lights, which burned cool, might be safer. She chewed this one over for a minute, and I raced ahead, asking rhetorically whether it might not just be time for something new in general. If we didn't like it, we could always switch back next year. I said this to sound reasonable but didn't expect such a thing to happen, as I knew that one view of my majestically tasteful handiwork would win everyone over for good.

This was about the time Mom spoke up. Mom usually stayed out of any fray involving Grammy and me, and I hadn't even been aware that she was listening to our exchange. But she loved Christmas, too, and had also, unbeknownst to me, been thinking of a change. To my horror, she produced a LaVerdiere's bag of her own containing a new set of lights. They were small, like mine, but colored like Grammy's, with a novel feature: they blinked. As she took the competing strand from the bag, she pointed out that her lights could be made to blink in alternating sections or all at once.

I was flummoxed enough to think that she had gone out and gotten new lights, and then it occurred to me that we had probably gotten them on the same excursion without my even noticing. Had she seen me in the Christmas decoration aisle and been inspired? Was she trying to trump me? I looked to Grammy to see how she was taking this not-quite tag team revolt. She had not even paused from unwinding lengths of old painted bulbs, despite the array of new options. She addressed my mother, but her message was meant to be global.

"You know your father likes these. You want to put on anything else, be my guest, but these are going on first."

Mom had no problem with that, so before I knew it, the tree was strung with both fat opaque bulbs in all the old colors and tiny see-through lights in a new palette that included pink and violet. I should have just called it quits right there, seeing as the tree already looked at war with itself, but I was stubborn and decided that at the very least, I could make the tree classier by adding the little clear bulbs I held in my hand. Let the other lights adorn the tree like so much costume jewelry; mine would be the equivalent of a string of pearls.

The next half-hour was an exercise in head butting. Mom had wisely left the room once her lights were up, leaving me to badger Grammy about which ornament went where. If she hung two satin-thread bulbs on the end of the same branch, I'd yelp that she was making things too "clumpy." If she hung all the plastic bells on the same side of the tree, I decried the clear imbalance. I began wordlessly moving the ornaments nearly as quickly as she hung them, which only increased her annoyance.

"Don't you have anything better to do than irritate me?" she snapped.

No, I thought to myself, I did not.

The boiling point was the tinsel. When I said I had *fresh* tinsel, Grammy looked at me as if she was seeing me for the first time.

"What on earth has got into you?" she asked me. "You think the tinsel is wrinkled? Tinsel doesn't go bad!"

I tried to paint a clearer picture of DAR Lady's strand-by-strand method, but Grammy had had enough. Throwing up her hands, she barked, "Do any old foolishness you want. It's none of my affair."

With that, she left me to my own devices, which was a clear victory for me, though it didn't feel very festive to have sent my grandmother stomping out of the room. I knew the results had to be perfect to have made the drama worth it.

An hour and a half later, I loathed tinsel with my whole heart. After only a few minutes I had realized that my game plan was a kind of madness: the individual placement of all five hundred "icicles." Yet once I understood the tedium of the task, I didn't dare stop, for the contrast between the painstakingly tinseled section and the rest of the tree would be naked. Not only would this be unappealing to the eye, but it would be perfectly obvious to Grammy that I had given up on a task she had scorned to begin with. My arms were trembling by the time I laid the last slip of tinsel on a branch near the bottom. My only source of consolation was that, as I wasn't planning to add garland, the tree really was finished.

Typically, we would have all gathered to light the tree as soon as it was dark. But just as we came together in the living room, we were startled by what sounded like a small explosion of some kind beneath our feet. I jumped; my brother said, "Holy moly," while Mom put a hand on her chest as if to still her heart. Grammy had just opened her mouth to venture a guess about the noise when the next explosion went off, followed by a third and then a fourth. She turned to Grampy with one of her darkest looks and jabbed a finger in his face.

"This is your fault!"

Grammy flew out of the living room and threw open the door to the cellar, disappearing from sight before anyone but Grampy had a clue what was going on. The longest wall of the earthen cellar beneath our house contained rows of canned pears, peaches, jams, strawberry-rhubarb sauce, pickled beets, mincemeat, and more. Grammy had been grousing that she never had room for all her canning, and so Grampy had set up an additional rickety wooden shelf, which would have been fine except for its location next to the furnace. Grammy doubted the wisdom of this idea, worried that overheating might cause ingredients to ferment or even combust, but Grampy told her she was just being a worrywart, like always.

Now, four quarts of applesauce had done just what she feared, heating so much that due to the pressure inside, the Mason jars finally burst their seals, sending the lids flying into the air like so many Wallendas. No one liked to be proven wrong by Grammy, who was not a bit shy about pointing out her correctness, but Grampy liked it least of all, having suffered this fate many a time in fifty-three years. He didn't exactly hurry down the stairs behind her to see the damage.

From the top step, I peered down to see what havoc exploding jars could wreak. It wasn't pretty: wet chunks of apple pressed cobwebs into earthen walls, and soupy liquid softened the dark soil floor. It was appleswamp now.

By the time the mess was cleaned up and Grampy had been thoroughly chastised, we all needed a little Christmas cheer. Ignacio did the honors of plugging the tree in, and then, well, we all just stood there a moment. Grammy chewed the inside of her lip, deciding how much to say, and Mom hazarded a tentative, "It's different." Grampy said what he always said, which was, "Well, good enough." It seemed as if everyone was intuitively (and uncharacteristically) trying to spare my feelings, but I just kept quiet.

I *hated* my tree.

It wasn't the fact that there were three kinds of lights on the tree. It wasn't that things weren't balanced enough—indeed, each ornament looked as if it had been marshaled into place like a soldier on parade. I had even achieved the same unified shimmer effect as the DAR Lady, so I couldn't blame my repulsion on failed tinsel application. No, the problem was that it didn't look like our tree at all.

This tree, the product of so much effort, was too even, too balanced. It looked absurd in our homey living room, where the entirely mismatched furniture was unified only by a host of hand-crocheted afghans. The absence of garland meant the tinsel took center stage, and it was so precisely applied that it appeared freakish. Any hint of playfulness and spontaneity had been replaced by stiff uniformity. It wasn't at all inviting.

The only thing reminiscent of Christmases past was the inclusion of the mismatched colored lightbulbs. Those lights were all I had to convince myself that the tree was not a complete failure—but then the blinking began. By accident or design, the blink setting had been left on the sectional option, which meant that first three feet of roping blinked on and off, followed by the next three feet, and so on, until the flashing got back around to where it had started—then started again. The living room pulsed nonstop in rainbow colors, lighting up and going dark like a small-town disco with only one special effect.

I wasn't the only one hating it. Despite having herself purchased the offending strands, Mom complained, "That gives me a headache something awful."

"Then stop it!" said Grammy sharply, still prickly about her newly apple-coated cellar walls. Grampy wasted no time in tinkering with the first bulb in the string, and the lights blinked their last, to everyone's clear relief.

I paused, then said the unimaginable in a rush, "Let's do the whole thing over."

It was late in the day, and the tree would surely have kept, but no one argued. There was something about this specimen that just sat poorly with us all, and starting from scratch seemed the perfect solution.

Grammy brought all our holiday tins into the room, and we denuded the tree between bites of divinity fudge and peppermint patties. Once we'd stripped it down to the now steady lights, we followed a merry random path in reassembling things. No one looked too closely to see where anyone else hung an ornament, and when it came time for tinsel, it fairly flew through the air as we tossed inelegant clumps at the branches. In the end, there was a general agreement that maybe the garland, at least, had outlasted its welcome, and it was returned to the cardboard box unstrung.

We were giddy by the time we stopped, a good hour after Grampy had abandoned our efforts. He was already snoring when we admired our handiwork. I knew that the DAR Lady would have been appalled, but this wasn't her house, and it wasn't her tree. Ours listed ever so slightly from all the poking and prodding it had endured, but it was cheerfully bright, even gaudy, a model of joyous abandon. Finally, as the old song goes, it was beginning to look a lot like Christmas.

10

A Hard Candy
Christmas

P roducts of the "Me Decade," kids of my generation were pegged as self-involved slugs who didn't care about the world. But you'd never have known that from the two youth groups I belonged to.

At my church, I was in Pathfinders, which is just like the Boy Scouts, except we included girls, our uniforms were the color of paste, and we had badges in things like "Witnessing." On Sunday nights, though, I went to Youth Fellowship, the much more casual teen program at the one other church in our town. I loved that both of the youth groups each ran annual charity events, which timed out with perfect synchronicity for me. First, I helped the Pathfinders collect canned goods for the poor between Halloween and Thanksgiving; after that, I joined the other church's Youth Fellowship first for a newspaper drive, then for tree decorating.

That all my charity work for the year was accomplished in the same ten-week period did not strike me as unusual; in fact, it just meant I was acting like a grown-up.

Of the three activities, my favorite was can collecting with the Pathfinders. Each year in the weeks surrounding Halloween, we Pathfinders were assigned mapped-out neighborhoods, which we papered in advance with fliers explaining what to give and what not to give. (Jell-O pudding packets, though not canned, were fine; raw hamburger, not fine). Then, on the date announced on the flier, we would return in uniform to get the paper bags filled with canned goods. Givers who did not actually want to deal with kids could simply set their bags out on the porch, and we'd snag them without even ringing the doorbell. (This always made me worry that we might accidentally snag the personal groceries of people who had just set their bags down for a moment to run inside and pee, though no such complaints were ever received.)

Though the food was collected around Halloween, it was not intended for distribution until Thanksgiving and Christmas. For that reason, clearly seasonal items like Pumpkin-shaped sprinkles and orange cupcake frosting were also discouraged. In the month before any poor person would be allowed to enjoy the bounty we'd harvested, the products sat in the church's food pantry. During these weeks, we kids were busy arranging the collected items into elaborate tableaux: making a peace symbol out of cans or building a skyscraper of Rice-A-Roni boxes. When we had finished constructing our box-and-can dioramas, we donned our uniforms and posed with our handiwork for snapshots.

Once our Great Pyramid of Campbell's soup cans had been preserved for posterity, the displays would be disassembled bit by bit as church members packed up baskets of goods to deliver to townsfolk who had been identified as living below the poverty line or suffering from some terrible circumstance. It felt quite noble, even poignant, to be involved in such an undertaking.

I was not, however, as enthusiastic about the Youth Fellowship newspaper drive. The stacks of newsprint were often dirty or wet and had to be tied with itchy twine, then hefted onto the back of a truck and driven off to be weighed at a recycling plant, which paid out what I remember as mere pennies per pound. This sequence offered all the things I didn't like: hard work, grime, and no photo opportunity. Even so, I did my part, cheerfully as possible, because I looked up to Roxie and Dick, the Youth Fellowship leaders, and because it meant I could spend more time with the friends I only saw on Sundays. But when the last bundle had been weighed, I was happy as a clam to move on to something more my speed: decorating the town Christmas trees.

Norridgewock was a small town. It had two intersections, but only one stoplight up at the top of the short main drag, which held a convenience store, a grocery market owned by the Libby family, and a beauty parlor next door owned by their flamboyant son Butch, a nickname roundly accepted as a joke. There were two churches, one public school, one church school, a little league field, two gas stations, a thimble-sized library, and an even smaller bank. Several doctors lived in Norridgewock, but only one practiced right in town, seeing clients in what had once been the parlor of her Victorian house. The sole employer of note was the shoe factory where Grammy had worked, and when its release whistle blew in the late afternoon, it yielded the only discernible traffic the town ever saw, which may be why there was also only one full-time cop. This was so not a town with a decorating budget.

It was up to the good will of Youth Fellowship then to provide any holiday accessories. Depending on the year, that might mean decorating a big tree in the main intersection, or down by the bank, or both. The town wasn't going to provide a generator to fuel any lights, and it wasn't as if the neighbors were offering to let us run an electric cord into their homes. Thus, the town trees were lightless displays, meaning that any arrangement of bulbs and garland would be completely invisible in the dark hours.

Then, someone came up with an idea that was both brilliant and a little trashy: cover the decorations in fluorescent paint so bright that the ornaments would seem to glow faintly in the dark at even the smallest graze of passing headlights.

Since there was no budget for bulbs either, the decorations in question were actually just Styrofoam cups. It was easy: just turn over a cup, poke a hook through the bottom (now the top), spray-paint the outside in a cheery hue, and voilà—a Christmas bell, albeit a soundless one. The only flaw, for some viewers, was our use of fluorescent colors. There is no such thing as a fluorescent Christmas color. Forget crimson and pine, or even fire engine red and Kelly green; we preferred the hot shades of rock posters and graffiti. Vivid lime, Gatorade yellow, and Barbie-lipstick pink—these bells didn't ring; they rocked.

It was a windy day that year as we hung the cups. Dick, the youth leader, was driving a town utility truck and had sent Blaine and Darryl, the oldest boys in the crew, up in the bucket. While they rose to the highest parts of the tree, the rest of us milled about sticking DayGlo bells wherever we could. One of the boys around my age leaned over and said, "You must really love this tree." The wind obscured the rest of his words.

"What?" I asked, trying to lean out of his spit zone.

"*Your* people *love* bright colors," he sprayed.

My people? It took me a minute to realize what he was saying. He didn't mean the people in my church, with whom no one was likely to associate fluorescent anything. He meant Cubans. And I could tell it was supposed to be a dig.

It was not a fun year to be half Cuban in rural Maine. The arrival of the Marielito refugees on the shores of

Florida had set off a wave of reflexive anti-immigrant sentiment that had shocked me. I was in York's Market one afternoon when the woman behind the counter said she'd seen "that spic kid" hanging out with his buddies on the corner. (The location of this corner didn't need specification: the town had only one.) It wasn't till she noticed me standing there and turned red that I even realized she was talking about my brother. Ignacio was a spic? Since when? I'd heard the term before, but I'd always thought it meant Puerto Ricans, which we weren't. And if Ignacio was, that meant I was, too. I didn't like the idea that I could be defined against my will in such a way.

Bizarre Cuban stereotypes had crept up everywhere. "You all like 'hot' food, right?" asked one of my classmates' parents, though the black beans and rice I loved in Miami weren't spicy at all. Another friend said, apropos of nothing, "You don't have black hair like a real Cuban," not that he knew any or had seen any of my cousins, most of whom were as fair as I was. Whereas just the year before it had seemed as if no one understood that I had a life outside the one in Maine, now people were curious about that part of me for all the wrong reasons. My actual relatives—Tia Fina and Tio Luis, middle-class homeowners sending their kids to college—were no match for the version my Maine neighbors collectively imagined them to be: loud-clothes-wearing, loud-music-listening hotbloods living off food stamps and the indulgence of Uncle Sam.

It didn't help that Ignacio and I were now living out part of that stereotype. Mom (who was not Cuban at all) got us by on food stamps and part-time work, having recently moved us out of Grammy's house and into a HUD apartment a half-mile away. The town drunk lived one door down in our building; he was prone to doing face-plants in the driveway, where he would lie asleep until the buzz wore off. In another unit, young marrieds were doing serious drugs to celebrate their new life as parents. The apartment complex wasn't a pretty place, but I didn't give much thought to it one way or the other; with so many activities at the two churches, I was rarely home. It had never occurred to me that our situation, based as it was on class and the limited opportunities of a depressed region, might play into anyone's notions of my race or heritage.

I considered how to reply to my fellow tree decorator. I could have pointed out that if he wanted to insult me by linking ethnicity to bright colors, he might first want to put down the hot pink bell in his hand. I could have said that this crazy tree, whose psychedelic hues were bold enough to scar your retinas, was the brainchild of Mainers, not Cubans. But I kept quiet. I just made a show of not answering.

"I can't hear you," I said, ducking around the tree.

He called out, but I shouted over him. *"I said, I can't hear you!"* He could think what he wanted, but like most people, I preferred to define myself.

As we hung the last bells, the passing cars honked at us, which we took to mean that we had done a fantastic job. With the finished tree resembling Christmas on acid, we went our separate ways. I wouldn't see these kids for another week, as they would return to their public school. I'd see all my own church school classmates again starting the next morning.

As it turns out, I didn't have to wait that long.

I was in the kitchen of our apartment putting away dishes when there was a knock at the door. This was a fairly rare occurrence as I didn't ever invite my friends to this dark place, with its low ceilings and windowless living room. The landlord, who was now dating my mother and noisily eating dinner with us every night, never really knocked so much as poked his head in to announce himself. Grammy didn't come over at all, figuring we could come to her.

The knock at the door was a surprise then, and I turned to look with an instinct that it would be bad news. In a way, it was. For when I opened the door, I found two of my church school classmates standing there. One held in her arms a big box, which I recognized immediately as a holiday basket. Of groceries. *For the poor.*

I didn't get out a word as my classmate spoke the very same line I had said to complete strangers in previous years.

"We just wanted to give you something to help make this holiday season a little easier."

A lot of things went through my head. The times I'd delivered the charity baskets—and make no mistake, that is what they were—I had noted the sagging state of the recipients' trailers or the forlorn appearances of their run-down farms, and I had felt kindly and beneficent, which is to say superior, the purview of the one bringing the groceries. I had not equated those homes, those people, with us. Yes, we lived on food stamps in a HUD apartment and wore a lot of second-hand clothes. But I had bought into the notion of poor people as shown on television: greasy, foul-mouthed smokers whose back porches were cluttered with beer cans. That didn't apply to us. Not even close.

But the evidence was before me. In my friend's grasp were the groceries I myself had collected expressly for the poor. If I accepted the box, I accepted the term. And I knew, without even looking, how empty the cupboards behind me were. I had no choice but to thank the girl and open my arms for this painful gift.

I shut the door shut behind her as she hurried back to her parents' car, ready to make more deliveries. I peered into the box, my mind quiet as the empty kitchen. Macaroni and cheese. Boxes of pudding. Stovetop Stuffing. We would eat these things, all of them, no question. Maybe we'd even forget their provenance.

It was work to stay cheerful. I hummed a tune that I considered inspirational: Dolly Parton's "Hard Candy Christmas," in which she lists possible ways to deal with a blue holiday. First, she suggests just dying her hair, but then she ramps it up, pondering moving so far away that people would lose track of her. The drab kitchen faded away as I imagined getting away from this apartment, this town, the boy who called me "Porker," and people who said "spic." I saw myself somewhere else, somewhere better—a city maybe, a place where I could be whomever I chose because nobody knew any different. And why not? If a hot pink bell that didn't ring could be a Christmas ornament, anything was possible.

When Mom woke up from her afternoon nap and stepped into the kitchen, she found me completely lost in thought, the box still unpacked.

"What's all this?" she asked.

"Christmas came early this year," I answered.

I reached into the carton and produced two packages of chocolate pudding mix. I knew they were her favorite.

II

Country of the Wicked Pointy Firs

"**S**cotty," I yelled, but he was so far above me, clinging to a forty-foot spruce, that he didn't hear. The December wind ate my words, but I tried again. "Scotty!" I shouted, my voice getting hoarse. "You have to stop!"

He looked down over his shoulder at me, raising his eyebrows questioningly. I saw the look on his face just about the time he understood what was going to happen next.

Some families make a tradition of going out to get their Christmas tree together. I knew a set of sisters in my school who always tromped out into the woods—and this being Maine, there were woods everywhere—to help their parents make the perfect selection. This sounded romantic to me, and I pictured a woodland scene right out of Disney, with sunlight shining off of icicles and perhaps a smattering of chipmunks and cardinals. But the eldest daughter confided to me that she thought the whole thing was a drag: her mom and dad would bicker about the sizes and shapes of the trees around them until their bored daughters were so cold that they had to stomp their feet to keep the blood moving.

Whether a tree comes fresh from the woods or is plucked from among the offerings at a local Boy Scout's Christmas tree stand, is there really any way to make the whole experience idyllic? If you've ever wrestled a wobbling spruce onto your car, trying to secure knots with frostbitten fingers, you know what I mean. Once you get it home, there's the issue of screwing the trunk onto the tree stand of choice without inadvertently fixing it into a tilted posture, thus having to start the whole process over again.

Maybe it was because the whole experience was so fraught with perils—chief among them losing one's holiday cheer—but my grandparents had never included Ignacio and me in any Christmas tree–gathering excursions. The first year after Mom moved us into our own apartment, we didn't even have a tree because the landlord said it would be a fire hazard, and my Mom, who was dating him at the time, didn't want to argue. But a year later, the landlord, who had by then dumped Mom and was trying to make nice, decided to let this rule slide for a season. This meant, for the first time ever, that I got to help pick out a Christmas tree.

I had no intention of buying one off a lot somewhere. For I was now a high schooler and that came with privileges, one of which involved trees. Riverview wasn't actually the local high school; instead, it was just a three-room church school that housed grades one to four in one classroom, grades six to eight in the next, and grades nine to ten in a third. (Juniors and seniors were out of luck; they had to look elsewhere for their education.) Once students made it into that ultimate classroom, they really ruled the roost, and that year, Scotty and I were among the elder statesmen. This meant we got to do the most exciting things, like digging around with our hands inside an enormous deceased cow from a nearby farm for biology. We also got to go on the most unusual field trips, such as our jaunt to a funeral home, where the mortician horrified us with his trocar, a big metal slushie straw for innards.

The most seasonal of the perks for those of us at the top of the totem pole was that we got to cut class to hunt for our own Christmas trees. Actually, it wasn't quite that naked, but it was true that the class day was shortened several times to allow us ninth and tenth graders the option of heading out into the school's surrounding woods to find trees for our families. This was both a privilege of our age and a fund-raiser; if our families were happy with the trees we'd chosen, they'd pay for them. Our parents felt good about supporting the school, and we kids felt even better about getting out of class.

Though Christmas trees were being farmed all around the school building, they were young, not to be harvested for years. The evergreens we could choose from stood in the woods far back on the school property, past the playground, beyond the fields, up above an unused sandpit. It would be a good fifteen-minute walk before we'd even reach the first stands that might offer up real possibilities. Being released from classes an hour early, then, made all the difference—not just in the hunt, but in the spirits of the would-be woodsmen.

When Mr. Carter asked who wanted to get trees that December afternoon, my hand shot up. This was my golden chance to find a tree for the apartment that would dazzle Mom and make the tree in Grammy's house look second-rate by comparison. Mr. Carter reminded us that we had to choose partners, no matter how many people wanted to go, because the school property extended for hundreds of acres. It was likely that even if we departed in a group, we would separate in the vastness at some point. The last thing the school needed was for some kid to get lost and never find his way back, freezing to death and totally ruining Christmas for all of us. Then, there was the possibility of an individual's sawing off her own limb accidentally and not having a freaked-out classmate nearby to run screaming back to school for help. No, it was clear, we needed tree buddies for this task.

That day, mine was Scotty. We'd been in school together for a decade, so long that it didn't really matter that we didn't have anything else in common. My actual best friends at the school were all girls—Debbie, Jenny, and Joy—but they tended to team up for tasks like this. The other two guys in the class were into ham radio and model rockets and science, which meant they might as well have been visitors from another planet. Scotty floated between these worlds on his own untroubled cloud of affability, a little goofy and a lot mellow. By age fifteen, when I'd known him for half my life already, my friendship with Scotty was like an old moccasin: so worn in, so comfortable, I was hardly aware of slipping into and out of it.

As we put on our coats, Scotty pointed out that I had no saw. This was true. I had ignored Mr. Carter's instruction that we must bring tools from home because the school simply didn't have a handy stash of a dozen hacksaws to hand out. (This was another era, a time before anyone ever imagined students passing their bags through metal detectors and facing pat downs by security guards.) I hadn't exactly forgotten, but Mom didn't have any tools, so I would have had to ask Grammy for a saw if I wanted one. And I knew where that would go, considering the miserable failure I had proven to be at helping her chop wood for the stove.

Whereas she could stand a piece of hardwood up on its end, tap it once firmly with the head of her axe, then cleave the thing neatly in two with a mighty second swing that left its halves spinning on the ground, my feeble attempts always involved lopsided blows bouncing off untroubled lengths of sugar maple until my arms went numb. I consoled myself that chopping a log and sawing a tree were entirely different things, but it wasn't worth asking Grammy's opinion on this score, so I didn't mention the saw to her at all.

Scotty, agreeable as always, seemed to accept that we would have to take turns with his equipment, and we set off. Scotty was a whippet of a boy, with long slender legs, and I had to hurry to keep up with him. Except for my huffing and puffing, we were silent for a good part of the walk, all of it uphill. But I was not the quiet type. I was Mr. Conversation, wanting to chat, chat, chat all the day long. As soon as we got to the edge of the woods, where we could slow down and poke about looking for our immobile prey, I started up, talking about a budding interest of mine: politics.

I had all kinds of newly hatched grievances involving President Reagan, not surprising for a boy living on welfare. I had even written him an angry letter to complain about his policies; to my surprise, the Gipper had ignored my sage advice and had instead responded with a hand-signed note praising me for my good attitude. This struck me as an outrage, but Scotty's eyes just kind of glazed over as I ranted on. What he finally said was, "You're funny, Dave."

To be fair to Scotty, I am guessing that not a lot of fifteen-year-olds in my town were obsessed with Reaganomics or much else political. The dominant passions of most rural kids my age—snowmobiling, for instance—left me cold. Every conversation like the one I was having with Scotty reminded me of my alien nature, so I thought it wise to remain mum for the rest of our hike.

I was well lost in my own thoughts when Scotty stopped and said, "How about this one?"

At first, I didn't see what he was talking about. We had walked so long that the sky was already taking on the grey-gold tinge of dusk. Around us mostly were towering blue spruce trees with a smattering of firs nestled among them. If you are from the heart of the city or a bone-dry desert, the differences in evergreens might not be obvious to you. But I had some firm opinions on Christmas trees (which is not surprising, as I had firm opinions on just about everything). For one thing, firs and spruces were acceptable tree choices, but pines were out of the question. With their long, spindly needles, pine trees were clearly not intended by God to hold ornaments. And a pine's pale green color is decidedly more fit for Saint Patrick's Day than for Christmas. This seemed perfectly obvious to me, but year after year, a pine tree or two showed up in the fund-raiser anyway, and it was all I could do to keep from physically intervening and saving potential buyers from such lame holiday also-rans.

Balsam firs were better. We always had balsams at home because they were cheap, but I didn't mind because their color was Christmas perfect. Plus, they boasted enough tensile strength to bear the weight of all but the heaviest ornaments. The more costly blue spruces were even better in that regard, with luxurious bristles that could hold up anything short of a barbell. A good spruce was also likely to boast a flawless shape, like an illustration on a Christmas card. Such virtues made it a crying shame to me that blue spruces were, well, blue. Yes, only faintly, more a tinge than a true shade, but once I saw one covered with red and green, it struck me as inescapably blue, which everyone knows is not a Christmas color.

That afternoon in the woods, the balsams before me were eight or nine feet tall, but all patchy, evergreen combs missing teeth. There was no way Scotty could want one of these gap-filled Charlie Brown specials. The blue spruces, on the other hand, were indeed majestic—too majestic. Towering fifty feet high or more, these monsters could've filled an entire room at their widest points, if a room that tall even existed. Trees like this were destined to stand in only one of three places: the White House lawn, Rockefeller Center, or right where they'd stood for a century already. Scotty couldn't mean one of these.

But that's exactly what he meant. "Do you see?" he said, looking to the top of the massive tree directly in front of us. It was so enormous that I had to step backward to get a clear view of the whole thing. Only then did I understand what Scotty was saying. The *top* of this monster was perfect. I mean perfect. Nothing is worse than a Christmas tree that looks stunted because the highest branches rise above where the top trails off, leaving an indentation where there should be a peak. Conversely, a top that is too long is nearly as bad; if the branches stop more than a foot below the crown, the tree takes on an unfortunate resemblance to a toilet brush. What you want is a tree that resembles a perfectly pointed cone, remaining evenly round as it narrows on its way to a sharp arrowhead tip, neither stubby nor spaghetti-like. Scotty noted the sleek triangular crown of the tree before us and paid it a high compliment in Maine vernacular. "It's *wicked* pointy!"

It was also wicked far away. Scotty's idea was to saw off just the flawless top eight feet of the tree. This poor spruce, having nobly endured decade after decade of Maine's harsh climate, was about to go from pointy to stubby at the whim of an enterprising fourteen-year-old—and I thought it was the most brilliant plan I'd ever heard. No young tree, still close to the ground, would ever match the lush perfection of the top of a stately older tree like this. Scotty was going to bring back the most impressive tree anyone had ever seen, blue or not. If we hurried, I could follow suit and lop off the gorgeous top of some ancient wonder myself.

First, Scotty had to climb the tree. He held the hacksaw in his teeth by the handle, which struck me as a smidge risky, but as he needed both hands to climb, he felt he had no choice. As he disappeared into the branches, it occurred to me that there was no way I felt like climbing several stories off the ground, with or without a saw. Since my two-story fall while snow-jumping years before, I had not climbed a thing. Chubby and perfectly able to envision my own horrible falling death, I realized I would not be replicating Scotty's feat, no matter how badly I wanted to go home with the best tree.

Scotty, on the other hand, was in his glory. He emerged, looking startlingly small and slight, less than ten feet from the treetop. With his legs wrapped around the trunk, and one hand holding on as well, he was finally able to take the hacksaw out of his mouth. He positioned the blade on the far side of the tree, then grabbed both ends, letting the teeth dig into the bark. This second grip on the trunk allowed him to lean back and ask for my opinion. "About here?" he shouted down, the wind in the trees not carrying his words very well. I gave him a thumbs-up and a big smile, hoping I didn't look as envious I felt.

As he set to work, it was getting colder by the minute. I stomped my feet a little to keep warm and started humming a song to amuse myself. The humming turned to singing, softly at first, and then, because I couldn't help myself, louder. My voice echoed through the trees around us, and I looked up to see whether Scotty was noticing. He was not. Even from a distance, it looked like he was sweating from the effort of sawing. Back and forth, back and forth. I was sure we were going to be there all night.

Forty feet up, Scotty was making headway as I belted out a chorus down below. The blade was inching closer to him slice by slice. Closer . . . closer. . . . And then I stopped singing at the precise moment I registered what I was seeing: Scotty was sawing towards himself, not away. And that meant, when the tree fell, it would take him with it.

"Scotty," I yelled, but he was too far above. The December wind ate my words, as I tried again. "Scotty!" I shouted, my voice getting hoarse. "You have to stop!"

He looked down over his shoulder at me, raising his eyebrows questioningly. I saw the look on his face just about the time he, too, understood what was going to happen next. With a hard snap echoing in the cold like the crack of a gunshot, the treetop let go of the trunk and leaned into Scotty's deeply startled embrace.

It takes a surprisingly long time for a kid to plummet forty feet with his new tree. My mind was racing much faster than Scotty was falling. *If he breaks his neck or his back, do I try to move him or leave him there, and will he end up in a wheelchair making paintings with a toothbrush held between his teeth? If he falls on the saw and it goes right through him, do I pull it out or leave it in? If he stops breathing, do I give him mouth to mouth, and if he wakes up right in the middle of it, will he misunderstand and punch me?*

The ground was too cold even to shudder with the impact of boy and tree, and the snow was too shallow to cushion their landing much. I didn't cry out for help, and I didn't even move for a moment. I just leaned forward, peering at the mass of blue-tipped branches for signs of motion. There was no movement in the pile of human and spruce limbs.

Could he be dead?

I became aware all at once that I was standing there in a daze, imagining the worst instead of actually helping. "Scotty," I whispered, breaking my own spell. "Can you hear me?"

No sound—not even easy wind and downy flake.

"Scotty?" I was cold all the way through.

I lifted the tree off him a little, startled to see his open eyes staring straight ahead. Whatever distant stars had filled his vision on impact, he finally registered me now. Still unmoving, he uttered one eloquent syllable: "Whoa."

I almost cried with relief, and I was irrationally tempted to kiss him. But I did neither. I just rolled the tree off and helped him sit up. I was still shaking, asking whether anything was hurt or broken, but his mellow Scotty-ness was already returning. "Did you see that?" he asked, laughing, as if I might have been doing something else.

"I thought you were going to die," I offered.

This gave him new pause for a moment. He just shook his head in wonder at the notion.

"Whoa."

With the tree hoisted onto our shoulders, branches slapping our faces, we began the trek back to the school. Our return journey felt a lot longer, burdened as we were, and we slowed considerably the closer we got to our destination. It was fully dark before we arrived. Thankfully, the light of the gymnasium revealed that the spruce was, indeed, still wicked pointy and not much dented by its tumble to earth. By the time his family came to collect him—and his prize tree—our adventure had become a tag team tale we could amuse people with, a funny bit about how far Scotty had gone to get the perfect specimen.

A classmate's family offered me a ride home, and I had them drop me off at the corner nearest my drab apartment building. I startled whistling "Sleigh Ride" as I made my way up the long dirt driveway, knowing that my mother always listened for my arrival. When I got inside and started stripping off my coat and boots, she greeted me, curious about my empty-handedness. "You didn't find a tree?"

"Nope," I said with a big grin. "But I have a story. And it's a good one."

12

Another Christmas Carol

I n fifty-eight years of marriage, my grandparents had never moved beyond the sleepy Kennebec Valley in Maine. For thirty of those years, they'd lived in the same house a short stroll from the homes of other relatives spanning three generations. By the time she was forty, my mother had spent all but five years of her life living within a mile of Grampy and Grammy, and there was, even then, constant talk of her moving back in. This was the kind of close physical proximity that keeps family ties strong.

It can also cause a young man to pack his bags.

There comes a time in a boy's life when he understands that the games and daydreams of his childhood have been telling him all along who he is meant to be as an adult. Sometimes, this realization only deepens his connection to the places and people surrounding him. But for me, it was clear: I couldn't become the person I wanted to be if I stayed where I was.

The first stop on my path forward was Union Springs Academy, a boarding school in upstate New

York, perhaps a surprising choice as it was six hundred miles away from my hometown. But a handful of kids from Maine were enrolled there, and their families carpooled, so I knew I could overcome the obstacle of the vast distance. More importantly, the school offered "work study" jobs, which meant, at least in theory, that a diligent student could earn his own keep without asking for help from, say, his retired grandparents and mother. I was determined to spend my last two years of high school there.

I hadn't warned my mother that I was making any such arrangements but instead let her assume I'd finish my education a little closer to home, at least somewhere in my own state. Wanting to avoid a confrontation for as long as possible, I kept mum about my plans until a few weeks before classes were to start. When I finally broke the news, I phrased it as a statement, not a question open for discussion. This hit her like a cold front: she braced herself, then leaned away from the chilly blast.

"What about me?" she asked, hurt and surprised. It was a fair question, but I already had a vision of myself as an academy boy living a whole new life and couldn't be dissuaded.

I didn't actually realize that when I left home, I would be leaving for good. I would spend my summers working at sleepaway camps, then go to college in Massachusetts. This meant I'd never again spend more than a week or so in my mother's house. I had prematurely settled into the pattern of adulthood, making my home elsewhere and only returning to see my family for the holidays. Full of pride at my personal reinvention, I thought of those early visits home as a kind of retreat from my progress toward the future. As condescending a teen as ever lived, I thought of going back to Maine for Christmas as an obligation, a charitable act for my family's sake more than my own.

By Christmas 1984, I was just one term away from graduation. When a classmate's family dropped me off in front of our apartment, I bore little outward resemblance to the kid who'd left home fifteen months before. Gone were my stiff Dickie work pants and arrow-front country-western shirts. My wardrobe now featured shiny black slacks and a half-dozen skinny ties. Standing in the dimly lit front yard, I was clad in my roommate's Members Only jacket, its band collar and snap epaulets defining me as a cool seventeen-year-old of the 1980s.

The internal changes were just as profound. Whereas I'd once listened to the same country music as my mom, I now preferred danceably suggestive pop songs like "Relax (Don't Do It)." I was beginning to see Mom and Grammy as *parochial,* an unflattering word I'd learned in English class and had applied to them because they stuck so close to boring little Norridgewock, while I was living in a place where I could run off to the mall for an Orange Julius or the latest album by The Cars. I was sure I had outgrown my family.

I hesitated before going inside. But I could only stand in the cold for so long. I pulled open the front door and stepped into the empty, unlit kitchen.

One light in the living room was all that kept the apartment from total darkness. Just as I was thinking that Mom could have at least left the tree plugged in for my arrival, I realized that there was no tree at all. In fact, there was very little sign of Christmas, aside from one limp poinsettia and a few cards taped to the refrigerator.

There was also no Mom, though her car was in the driveway. When she wasn't waiting at the kitchen door, I expected she'd be ensconced in her usual seat in the living room watching television. But her easy chair was empty, save for a crocheted afghan. She wasn't in the bathroom either. Her bedroom door was closed, with no sliver of light shining underneath. It wasn't even eight o'clock, yet it appeared she'd already gone to bed. Her youngest son had just traveled hundreds of miles, and she hadn't even bothered to wait up for him.

Whatever, I thought.

In my old room, I yanked the beaded metal cord that turned on the overhead light and laid my suitcase on my brother's old bed. With me away at school and Ignacio in the Marines, the room no longer felt lived in. The same threadbare Indian blanket bedspreads covered our beds, but all the posters had been taken down, and Ignacio hadn't left behind so much as his Frisbee or ball glove. I could have been unpacking my things in a motel, except a motel room would have at least had its own television and curtains.

As I sorted my clothes, my mind was far away, mentally replaying scenes from academy life, especially my star turn in the school musical. Having been somewhat obsessed with *A Christmas Carol* since I was eight, I had often before daydreamed scenarios in which I might someday get to play old Ebenezer before an adoring crowd. My lifetime of Scrooge envy had finally been rewarded a week earlier at school when I'd gleefully hammed it up as the crotchety character, and though the production was low budget, it came with everything I had dreamed of: singing ghosts, an adorable Tiny Tim, and oodle-kaboodles of stage time for me. The only thing missing had been my family.

In my heart of hearts, I had known it was unreasonable for me to expect Grammy, Grampy, and Mom to come so far. My grandparents were in their seventies, and Mom seemed stuck in a cycle of ill health. Beyond that, it wasn't their fault I had so boldly decided to go to school three states away. And yet I'd held out hope that they would show up to surprise me anyway, the kind of happy twist you might see in an after-school special. When some of the other parents from Maine did show up, the absence of my family, fair or not, had stung.

Just a week removed from the applause that greeted our show's finale, I found the stillness of mom's apartment—and the lack of her greeting—hard to take. I needed to get out, if only for a few hours. But first I'd replace my old sneakers with my cool Capezio lace-ups from school; making the switch instantly made me feel better, more like the self I wanted to be and not the small-town kid of my past. Pulling on my jacket, I left Mom's quiet apartment behind.

December nights in Maine are not warm. Though the temperature might peak at a whopping twenty degrees in the full light of day, the mercury often drops below zero after dark, and the wind chill can plummet into the negative double digits. When I set out on the quarter-mile walk to Grammy's neighborhood, it became immediately clear that a Members Only jacket offered only slightly more protection from the elements than a Bounty paper towel. My wafer-thin shoes were worse: the soles were so slippery that I was at serious risk of breaking an ankle on the ice; even if my bones survived the trip, I might well lose a toe or two to frostbite.

My destination was my old church, which sat directly across the street from my grandparents' house. Neither site promised much excitement, but I figured someone would at least be around to greet me. Just a few days before Christmas, it was the night before

Grammy's annual cantata, and I knew she'd be at church putting her tired choir members through their paces one last time. When I reached the street, Grammy's house was dark, except for a porch lamp and the colored lights of the Christmas tree in the living room window. But the church stood fully aglow across the way.

When I slipped into the back row of the sanctuary, the men of the choir were dragging out their big number, and Grammy was desperately pounding out the rhythm on her wooden lectern in a valiant attempt to speed them up. She shot me a look as if to say, "Don't distract my choir!" and kept goading the men along.

Despite having sung this cantata with the choir in previous years, I wasn't expected to join them in their pews up front. Grammy had already warned me over the phone that if I couldn't come to all the practices, it would throw everything off to have me jump in so late. Instead, she suggested I sing a solo, saying she'd fit my number in just before the finale. Because that prime slot was usually filled by my aunt Marion, who had the best voice in the whole church, this might have been a kind of honor, but it was not in Grammy's nature to say such a thing. She simply admonished, "You make sure you practice before you get home."

She needn't have worried on that score. My academy was full of girls who played piano, and I'd pressed most of them into service as I rehearsed my piece over and over. I had chosen a Christian pop song with the deceptively reverent-sounding title "Emmanuel." When I had announced my selection over the phone, Grammy paused a moment and asked if I meant an old carol with a similar name. "Sort of," I said, knowing full well that the austere minor-key hymn she was thinking of bore no resemblance to my song. She let this go, and though I knew I was setting myself up for a conflict, I did too.

Though "Emmanuel" begins gently enough, it gets rocking by the third line. Forget the waltzing ditties of the cantata, the solo I was planning involved my belting out my best impression of Peter Cetera vocals over a galloping keyboard line worthy of Mannheim Steamroller. In retrospect, this music was only slightly more edgy than Muzak, yet this was the kind of number that wowed the crowd every time at the academy.

On the long ride home, I had considered how my solo would go over in Norridgewock. Mom would like anything I sang, and I was banking on the school-aged kids' being into it as well. Some of my classmates' families were pretty progressive, and I even figured a few other churchgoers might find it a welcome relief from thirty years of the same shopworn tunes. But I knew that Grammy wouldn't like it one bit.

Why do a number I was so sure she'd disapprove of? Why does a seventeen-year-old do anything? Independence. I figured if I had already left home and was putting myself through school, I could do whatever I wanted. It would be the new me singing my heart out during the Christmas service, and Grammy could like it or lump it.

Something in me was picking a fight.

When rehearsal ended and the choir members drifted off to see if their very cold cars and trucks would still start, Grammy asked if I wanted to come over to the house for a bit. She held my arm as we crossed the icy road, and I was struck by how tiny she felt, a mere ghost of the imposing woman who had raised me.

As she tiptoed into her room to get her housecoat, I stayed out on the enclosed porch to stoke the fire in her woodstove. Watching embers pop and fade, I almost held my breath—being around Grammy always made me defensive. On the one hand, she had done much of the heavy lifting in raising me, and her prompting—Do your homework! Practice your music!—allowed me to excel at the academy. On the other hand, she had never been one of those soft, touchy-feely grannies; she was instinctively prone to criticism, not praise.

The first time I got all A's, her only response was to note that one grade was actually an A–. I tried to shrug that off like she hadn't scored a blow, but she had. In fact, I spent so much time convincing myself I wasn't trying to please her that I couldn't admit to feeling hurt when she inevitably failed to express pride in my achievements.

I pulled up a chair at the card table below the picture window my brother had once crashed through on a sled. The table was covered with church bulletins for the next day's service—but thankfully no bills. Every time I came home to visit now, Grammy would make a tableau of all her utility bills and wonder aloud, in barely rhetorical form, how she was going to keep up. To her way of thinking, anyone who could afford boarding school must be able to help out the family as well. Seeing as I was by this point $1,000 behind on my tuition payments, I disagreed.

Grammy padded out onto the porch now and said, in deeply uncharacteristic fashion, "How about you give your grandmother a hug?" She raised her cheek for a kiss.

For Grammy to initiate an embrace instead of just accept one meant something was up. She raised the anxiety level by asking me to turn off the overhead light, saying it felt too bright. A small lamp next to the card table would have to do, its glow forming a small circle around us. Once she was settled into her rocker and I in my chair, she let me in on the deal.

"Your mother hasn't told you, but she's very sick."

My first thought was that Mom was always sick. She had been hospitalized three times in the previous two years, always collapsing from a vague mix of chest pain, fatigue, and body aches. Even when she wasn't in the hospital, she tired easily and was often depressed, so I had never thought of her as well in the first place. But the word "very" in Grammy's description caught me short.

Systemic lupus erythematosus, according to Mom's doctor. The lupus was making Mom's whole immune system go into overdrive, wearing itself out as it fought off invisible threats. The problems that had long defined my mother—an inability to be in the sun too long, a predisposition to the blues, poor memory, a constancy of physical aches and pains—were the hallmarks of her disease.

I was shamed to discover that Mom hadn't gone to bed early that night because she didn't love me; her heavy new medications made it impossible for her to stay awake much past sundown. The more detail I heard, the less I wanted to take in. Though the toll of lupus could be as simple as unpleasant rashes, it could also be as dramatic as kidney failure. Or worse.

It is a useless thing to accuse the bearer of bad news of not bearing it soon enough, but I did anyway.

"Why didn't anyone tell me?"

Grammy raised her chin and it was immediately clear that she was seeing me as the callous teenager I was.

"Your Mom thought you should know, but I wouldn't let her call," she said, an edge creeping into her voice. "You were away at school and couldn't have done anything about it, so there was no point in making you sick with worry."

I was primed to argue with this logic like a little kid—hardly the behavior of a young man of the world.

But she spoke first. "We knew that being in that musical thing was a big deal for you, and we didn't want to spoil it." I shut my mouth. "I said to your mother, 'Let him have his night. There's plenty of time to tell him later.'"

She had, rightly, understood that my knowing would have been a burden, and not knowing was the only relief. But now the spell had been broken, so we simply sat together for a while, both of us looking out the window at all we couldn't see.

In the morning, Mom was up before me, and the first thing she said was how badly she felt about having been asleep when I came in. (I was pretty sure I felt worse for having held it against her, not that I could say so.) Her face was pale, her eyes watery, and she sat at the kitchen table, one arm resting heavily on the Formica top for support. I could see that she was worried about how to tell me what Grammy already had, and I let her off the hook. She seemed worried that my atypical quietness meant I was taking the news hard. She flailed about for the right words to make it sound better and landed on this excellent summary of illness in general: "I just need to feel good again, and then it'll be fine."

As I got ready for church, I decided I didn't want to wear the flashy jacket and the narrow leather tie I had packed after all. The solemnity of events called for something a little more old-school. In my room at home, I had kept only a couple of dingy-looking dress shirts and some very wide ties of 1970s vintage. I had no choice but to dress like someone on MTV and hope that I didn't look too cavalier as a result.

Mom seemed to approve.

"I saw on TV that skinny ties had come back. They remind me of when I met your father. Everyone had them." She smoothed mine down and shook her head. "Though they weren't made of leather then. How on earth do you tie this thing?"

I was so relieved that my outfit spawned nostalgia and not shock that I even let her button the collar on my shirt and pull up the knot of the tie, though this would have instantly marked me as a nerd anywhere else.

"You'll look good for your solo."

My solo. I had forgotten about it entirely. There was no way in this world that I could get up in front of my ill mother and start a feud with Grammy that would surely sour the day with tension, adding to Mom's woes. Beyond that, I was seeing Grammy in a different light than I had just days before. All the time I had been gearing up to prove to her that I was my own man, she had been protecting me from afar so that I could be just that.

I needed to change course, but I couldn't tell Grammy, who would naturally ask why. When Mom and I arrived at the church, I pulled the pianist aside and said I wasn't going to perform the song for which I'd given her the sheet music just the night before. When she asked what I was going to sing instead, I didn't have a good answer.

"I'll just sing something a cappella," I stammered.

Her eyes widened at the word "something," and I improvised, impulsively naming an old spiritual Mom liked that I knew all the words to. I pretended it was no big deal, but the pianist didn't seem convinced. I wasn't either.

Just as Grammy led her choir from their front pews to the pulpit, Mom and I crowded in next to Grampy on the very last pew in the back corner of the sanctuary, where his annual tape recording of the holiday service would not distract anyone. The cantata that followed was a crash course in emotional reckoning, though it was the memories, not the melodies, that worked on me. One song made me think of the year my voice broke and I finally got to sing with the men; another brought to mind the time I had been cast as one of the three kings only to flee when I flubbed my verse. When it was time for the ladies' trio number, somebody new was singing the part my mother had always sung before. Now, Mom was sitting next to me. I put my arm around her to reassure myself that she was still there.

When it was time for my song, I climbed the carpeted steps to the pulpit and took a deep breath. "Sweet little Jesus boy," I began and found myself on the verge of tears. I focused my eyes on the old church clock high on the back wall, fearful that making eye contact with anyone would cost me my composure. How many Christmases had my family played this carol on the record player without my ever feeling the sting of the lyric "Our eyes was blind, we couldn't see"? Like any kid, I had simply assumed my family's presence to be permanent; they were something to shuck off when I was ready, sure that they would still be there whenever I liked. Now I was beginning to understand that this just wasn't true.

It hadn't been sheer impulse alone that led me to pick a song so ripe with remorse; my heart knew that what I really wanted to do was apologize. The song was all I could offer, and I gave it everything I had.

When I finished, the last note hung in the air a bit, before a chorus of hearty amens. I looked to where I'd been sitting and saw that Mom had tears in her eyes; I looked to the front pew of the choir rows and saw that Grammy was snuffling softly into a tissue. She didn't look up at me, and I didn't try to catch her eye. As I returned to my seat, the pianist sounded the notes of the final number, and Grammy motioned for the choir to rise. Just then, a loud plastic click announced that Grampy's tape recorder had just stopped, *before* the cantata was actually over, for the third year in a row.

"Sugar tit," he muttered under his breath, using his strange favorite epithet. Only Mom and I could hear him swearing, and we tried not to laugh.

After the service, we ate dinner together as a family at Grammy's house. (Grammy insisted we call the noon meal "dinner," not "lunch," which she thought of as something carried in a bag.) We all took our customary seats. Grampy sat at the head of the table, and Mom at the foot, with Grammy and me next to each other on one side. My brother's chair across the table sat empty, and I suppose I could have moved over there to balance things out, but that would've felt wrong, like an erasure of Ignacio's place. Doubtful we'd ever assemble this way again, I didn't want to cede more ground to the march of time that was already changing the shape of our family.

Grampy fiddled with his tape recorder until he had the cassette rewound to the beginning of the cantata. This, too, was ritual, letting Grammy hear the results of her efforts from start to finish without the pressure of performance. Some parts we listened to closely, and others we talked over, passing the crock of baked beans and the hunks of homemade bread that we had eaten after church every week for years. The effort of sitting through the morning's service, then staying for the family meal, began to tire Mom. I knew we'd have to head back to the apartment soon, carrying slices of pie on paper plates wrapped in foil.

When the tape got to my solo, Grammy put down her fork and then waved as if to shush us all. She closed her eyes to listen, with her chin up and one hand covering her mouth. I can't say how I sounded on the tape for I was focused entirely on my grandmother. Her face, which had once seemed so severe to me, had softened into a cascade of deep lines. Her fingers, once dreaded for the fierce pinch they could inflict on a boy's ear, looked thin now, and trembled a little against her pale lips. Conversation had stopped entirely, and all eyes were glued on Grammy's rapture. I could hear her breathing. We all could.

When the song ended, she looked me straight in the eye and said, "That was the best you've ever done." And then she said something I had waited to hear ever since I had come to live with her at age four.

"I'm so proud of you."

Everyone understood that this was a moment. Mom brightened a little, and Grampy said, "Well, good enough!"

I had no words, so I threw my arms around Grammy to hug her fiercely. And she let me.

Through the door to the living room, I could see the glowing Christmas tree. Knowing Grammy as I did, I was pretty sure a wrapped pair of socks waited under the tree for me, and maybe a little something else. But it didn't really matter. We had already exchanged our gifts.

ACKNOWLEDGMENTS

Memory is a funny thing—you can think of an event a certain way your entire life only to discover you are conflating details or mixing up stories. To keep a volume of tales from decades ago as truthful as possible, I pressed my loved ones into service as human lie detectors. My brother read chapter after chapter and helped me keep the details sharp and on the money, while also providing a new lens for seeing old things; we may have bonded more over this book about our childhood than we actually bonded while living its events. Thanks also to Mom, whose memory is spotty but whose tending to the family photo albums has been flawless, which gave me a repository of helpful evidence. My cousins Glenice and Adrienne each vetted my recollections of the Ambrosia chapter, and I thank them for taking that trip down memory lane.

Writing a book about childhood highlighted for me how many grown-ups made a difference in my life through their expressions of love, encouragement of my talents, and acceptance of my quirks. Some of them are referred to in the book and some are not, but I must pause to thank them: Martha Howard, Betsy Mc-Grath, Leroy Jones, Renee Perry, John Carter, Dick and Roxie Wallace, Betty and Richard Luther, Brenda Closson, Carol Otis, Geri and Charles Zacharias, and Orinetta Spooner (who never knew she saved my life). Grammy, a colorful character in life—and a dear one—is no longer with us, but this book would never have been written without her influence on me.

Continual thanks to Wendy, Kate, and the whole gang at Da Capo, who know how to make a writer feel not just supported but lifted up; every author should be so lucky. Lastly, the completion of this volume was made possible because I have the world's best hus-band, who made many trips to farms and play-spaces with our beloved daughter while I wrote. The two of them are the best gifts anyone could ask for.